THE BLACK WOMAN'S GUIDE

TO BEAUTIFUL, HEALTHIER HAIR

IN *6 WEEKS*!

The 2003 Edition

THE BLACK WOMAN'S GUIDE

TO BEAUTIFUL, HEALTHIER HAIR

IN *6 WEEKS*!

The 2003 Edition

HAVE THE HAIR OF YOUR DREAMS!

An EASY At-Home Regimen
You Can Start TODAY!

Carolyn Gray

Life Changing Publications, LLC
Clifton, Virginia

The Black Woman's Guide
To Beautiful, Healthier Hair In 6 Weeks!
The 2003 Edition

Copyright © 2003 by Carolyn Gray
Publisher: Life Changing Publications, LLC
          Clifton, Virginia 20124

Second Edition

ISBN 0-9665171-1-3

Library of Congress Control Number: 2003097043

Cover Photos (front and back) courtesy of © The Picture People, Photographer Eric Cales
Portraits shown on pp. 87, 118, & 130 are courtesy of © The Picture People

Book orders may be sent to : LCPP&S, LLC
          5746 Union Mill Road, PMB 495
          Clifton, VA 20124

E-mail may be sent to LifeChgPub@aol.com
Visit www.blackwomansguide.com for online ordering and additional information.

Printed in the United States of America

~·~·~~·~·~·~

Publisher's Note

·~·~·~~·~·~·

The intent of this book is to present the author's ideas and perceptions about black hair care and some of the best, least expensive, products available for that purpose. **The author is not a licensed hair professional** and *does not claim to have the best plan for every woman's hair.* Her goal is to share her own personal six-week shampooing and conditioning regimen, daily hair care routine and styling tips, with the names of products included for each. **Although specific product names are mentioned, the publisher in no way endorses the use of one product over another.** *The advice and recommendations in this book are strictly a reflection of the author's opinions, views and experiences with the products and techniques mentioned herein.* There are no guarantees that you will experience the same results as the author or other readers, and it is very possible that you may find success with products not mentioned in this book. *Remember it is your right to select products based on your own preferences and beliefs, and you have the right to disagree with the views and opinions of the author.*

However, if you have any serious questions or concerns regarding the products recommended in this book, please contact the product manufacturers directly or get approval from appropriate medical or cosmetology professionals. Keep in mind that this book, as was the first edition, is written from a consumer's perspective – a consumer (*the author*) who has had wonderful results with most of the products mentioned in this book.

Also, on a more important note, *if you experience any type of irritation from any of the products mentioned in this book, as you use them according to the manufacturer's directions, stop using the product(s) immediately.* However, if you need medical advice or attention for your hair, scalp or skin, you should contact a dermatologist or your personal physician immediately.

•~•~•~~•~•~•

Carolyn has done it again in her latest edition of the Black Woman's Guide to Beautiful, Healthier Hair in 6 Weeks! This guide is packed with helpful hints, tips, and examples of how to achieve great looks and manage your hair the health way. It's a "must buy" for every woman who wants to have gorgeous hair.

Sista girl, I'm so very proud of you, keep reaching for your dreams!

Love,
Roz

•~•~•~~•~•~•

Dedication

One day I was out for a walk and a beautiful black sister called to me from her car. She wanted to know where I got my hair done, so I asked if she meant where I got my relaxer done? She said, "No, I mean where did you get your tracks put in?" We laughed as I told her that it was my hair, and I gave her the name of my stylist. Although it was an honest mistake, I don't feel that my hair is long enough that anyone should think that it is not real. As I remember this young woman and other women who have written me about their hair struggles, and as I look at black magazines filled with weave and wig ads, I sometimes get sad and have often wondered why it seems so hard for us? For too many of us the process of maintaining and growing our hair can all too often be a frustrating experience. I have been there, and I think I have made almost every hair mistake there is to make! However, as the Lord has helped me find a way out of so many of my hair troubles, I feel the need to share what I have learned as I get closer to reaching my goals. So this book is written for any sisters who have ever been frustrated, confused or discouraged where their hair is concerned. I dedicate this book to all of you, especially those who have written me over the years. I want you all to know that we can reach any goal we put our minds to, hair or otherwise! Our hair can be beautiful and healthy. It can also grow long if that is what we choose. So regardless of your goal, I say GO FOR IT, and I know with God's help you can reach it!

•~•~•~~•~•~•

Acknowledgments

As before, I must thank the Lord for inspiring me to write this book and for giving me the drive, ability and opportunity to complete it. Also, thanks for the trials and tribulations you *allowed* me to go through with my hair – without them, this book would have never been written.

I also want to thank my wonderful husband and sons (Christian & Evan) for being patient and supportive as always. *I love you more than you'll ever know.*

I also have to thank my cousin and sister-in-law, Rosalind Blocker and Pamela Gray-Williams, for being positive *sounding boards* for some of my goofiest ideas. Everyone needs someone to listen to their ideas, and I have really appreciated the outlet and your creative input. I also look forward to working with you both on future projects!

Finally, I would like to thank the wonderful readers of my first book who took the time to write me with such positive, genuine feedback. It is such a blessing to know the work that you do actually helps others, and your testimonials and kind words were the reason I wrote this book!

•~•~•~~•~•~•

CONTENTS

FOREWORD

As I have said before every woman wants beautiful, healthy hair, and we as black women are no exception. However, collectively, we do more to harm our hair than any other group of women. Because our hair is typically coarse and kinky, we think that it can withstand any sort of treatment or abuse. Many would be surprised to know that our hair can be pretty fragile and in need of just as much TLC (I am sure you know, but I mean **T**ender **L**oving **C**are) as other types of hair, if not more. However, even when our hair is pulled so tight by braids/extensions that we get a headache, or our hair sizzles from the heat of a curling iron, or our scalp burns from relaxers, if the finished product looks good we assume that no harm has been done. Unfortunately, many of us don't even realize that we are causing long-term damage to our hair and scalp. Also, because there may not be immediate evidence of damage, other than dryness, chronic breakage and split-ends or receding hairlines, we often continue our chosen form of abuse. We all have a weakness or *form of abuse* that we must guard against (e.g., overuse of curling irons, frequent use of blow dryers, infrequent shampooing and conditioning, rough combing/brushing, tight/heavy braids and extensions, or use of glues and bonding agents, etc.) – *everyone struggles with something*. However, if these offenses are combined with the use of harsh chemicals to relax and color our hair, it can often lead to weak, unhealthy hair.

For those of you that didn't read my first book, I will admit again that I abused my hair for most of my adult life with frequent heat styling and blow drying, infrequent shampooing and conditioning, rough handling and going from stylist to stylist. My *reward* was dry, brittle hair that would not grow past my shoulders without split-ends. Many people seeing my before and after pictures assume that I must have always had long hair. *Believe me, I didn't.* When I was fourteen my hair was shoulder-length and full, but things went down hill from there. No one ever taught me how to take care of my hair, and I could not afford regular visits to a quality salon. Most of the time my hair was a damaged, unmanageable mess. The only hair advice I ever really remember getting was to grease my scalp with Afro Sheen (you remember the green grease?), and I even remember picking shampoos based on TV commercials (e.g., Head & Shoulders, Prell, etc.). I don't remember anyone ever mentioning getting ends trimmed or deep conditioning until I was in college. However, by that time I was growing out an asymmetrical bob (it was the 80's) that I got out of frustration.

Since I couldn't get my hair to grow longer, I started teasing it to create fullness (I got the idea from looking at photos of Diahann Caroll's hair). This was about the time when Oprah became really popular and started wearing styles where her hair stood high on her head. I started wearing a similar style – hot curling (*often twice a day*) and then teasing it so it would stand up. Do I even need to say that split-ends and breakage were a major and constant problem for me from then on? *Every* time I went to a stylist, they would say, "You have split-ends," and trim away any growth I had acquired. This frustrating cycle went on for many years. Although I tried every product I could find that claimed to prevent or fix split-ends and breakage, n*one of them helped me grow my hair beyond my shoulders – I was stuck.* The only times that my hair would get longer than shoulder-length were times that I was either pregnant or decided not to have my *split-ends* trimmed. However, after my second pregnancy, when my hair immediately went back to the pre-pregnancy length, I decided that once and for all I was going to grow my hair down my back *without split-ends!* The problem became "how was I going to do it?"

Wouldn't it be neat if there was a "hair doctor" that could write out a customized hair care prescription for us, telling us what products to use and how often? Why can't stylists be trained to do that? I used to fantasize about some *dream* stylist who would come along and fix all of my hair problems. However, after going from stylist to stylist, some very expensive, with often disappointing results, I realized *that the answers I was seeking begin at home, not with the stylist.* As a result, I started looking for books and magazines that could recommend products **and** give me step-by-step instructions on how to use them to reach my goals.

I did find some hair care books that were pretty good, but they mainly told me about my hair's structural makeup, its texture, how to cut, color and style it, but provided no tangible details on how to actually **take care of it** on a day-to-day basis. *That's what I needed* – I know everyone has different needs, but I needed someone to really break it down for me! I didn't care about the difference between the cuticle and the cortex, whether my hair was type 4a or 4b (it's sad, but *I still don't*). I only wanted to know what reasonably priced shampoos and conditioners I should use to get my hair healthy and looking good. How could I get my hair to grow longer? How could I save time in the mornings on styling? How could I minimize split-ends and breakage? How could I create some of the serious hairdos I saw ladies wearing on TV and in movies without burning my hair up with a curling iron or spending all day in a salon? That's what I was *talkin' about – I was not really trying to hear the scientific stuff,* which is funny coming from a person who studied electrical engineering for the first 3 years of college! I just wanted the information, and then I wanted to run to my local beauty supply store **and** *get started immediately*!

I was really surprised to find that other sisters were out there looking for the same thing – *someone to buy and try the products first and then tell which ones actually work*! I started off this "buying and trying" phase with only my hair in mind, but when I saw that I was not by myself in this quest for knowledge, I got really excited. Because I love to write, I started making notes on my evolving hair care regimen so I could remember it and so it would be easier to share with others. Next thing you know, it turned into a 15-page *essay* called "*6-Weeks without a Blow Dryer!*" I know that is so corny (*fortunately an old co-worker pointed this out*), but I was just so excited that I had come up with a way to air dry my hair straight, *without* using a blow dryer. I had never heard of anyone showing us how to do that before, so I wanted to share it with everyone I knew! I started off with friends at MCI, and they were so interested that I started sharing other information from my regimen. My growing excitement was fueled by the results I could see in my own hair *and* in those who tried my techniques. So one night while I was working really late at MCI, my cousin and I discussed putting all I was learning in a book, *even though I had never written a book before.* It is so funny that I had been praying, asking God for a topic for my first book, and here it was…

This was the real start of my journey to have healthier, longer hair, and I have learned that it really is a *journey* – a life-long one at that. You never really *arrive* or get to a point where you can say I don't have to worry about my hair any more. If you stop "walking" (*doing the healthy things you know to do* like going easy on the heat, deep conditioning, etc.), you will see the effects on your hair – sometimes it is so gradual, that you don't see changes until you wake up one morning, wondering what the heck happened? How do I know? Because in my journey since the first edition of this book was published in 1999, I have done a whole *lotta* walking, and there has been some half-stepping on my part at times. Sometimes I have looked in the mirror and actually thought, "You big dummy – *what were you thinking*?" However, as I had my own personal hair mishaps and did even more research, I think I am back on the right path, a little smarter and my hair a lot healthier. As a result, I finally feel I have enough new information to share that other sisters can relate to and hopefully benefit from in their own journeys.

That is what this book is about, me *sharing my latest personal hair experiences.* Does this now make me a hair care expert? **Definitely not!** Being considered an expert in this field has never been my goal. This is one of the reasons you will never hear me talking a lot about the chemistry or science of our hair. For me, my interest is just not that deep, and there are so many talented writers out there that have already covered these subjects at length. *I am just a writer who was looking for a topic to write a book about, and coincidentally, I was going through a hair struggle at the time, so this became my topic.* The only reason I am writing this second, *and probably final*, edition of this book is because of the remarkable interest sisters have shown in the first book and the wonderful, touching testimonials I have received. As a Christian woman, I had been looking for a ministry to exercise my gifts for writing and encouraging people, and this hair care "*thing*" (the book, the website, e-mail advice, newsletters and now hair care products) became an outlet for me to do just that. However, I must admit that many times I do feel tempted to forget about writing on hair care and just focus on the many other books I plan to write, *keeping my hair care struggles/information to myself.* Fortunately, every time I thought of doing this, an e-mail would come in to make me want to keep sharing the good, the bad and the ugly details of my hair care journey. *This is where you find me now…*

FOREWORD

The objective of this book, as with the first edition, is to help you develop **your own** personal hair care regimen that you can follow year after year, modifying as needed, to help your hair look its very best and to be in the best possible condition. This book not only tells you what I do and how often, but it also gives the names of reasonably priced products *that work*, where to find them and step-by-step instructions on how to use them. Please note that the product recommendations made in this book are not based on any type of sponsorship from the manufacturers – they are based on my own personal experiences and results. I have personally used *every* product recommended in the *Six-Week Regimen* (Chapter 3) and in the Daily Hair Care section (Chapter 5), with phenomenal results. My hope is that you will experience the same incredible results I do, using the products I have tried or those of your own choosing and reach *any* hair goal you may have!

Chapter 1

INTRODUCTION

If you are like me, most of the times you don't want to go through problems or have anything go wrong for you, and when they do, you are thinking like, "*Why God?*" However, I am finding that every time I go through something painful or annoying in my life, I usually wind up being able to rise from it and share with or help someone else, which makes me say, "*Okay God, I see why now.*" *This time is no exception…* Over the last few years, I have experienced dryness, breakage, raggedy ends, slow growth and thinning, *even after I thought I had arrived*. However, after working to overcome these conditions and getting so many requests for a second edition, I decided to share my personal "findings" with all of you in what I hope is my last book on hair care. What I have learned may not be the 100% answer for everyone, but I am sure that in my story you may find *something* that you can relate to or benefit from in your own personal journey or regimen.

My personal struggles motivated me to find ways to correct or treat problems such as dryness, thinning and raggedy ends. *Nothing motivates you more than when a problem hits home*! In trying to solve my own problems, I found new products, tricks and routines to help me **re-revolutionize** my Six-Week hair care regimen. I have shared some of this information in the form of newsletters (*The Black Hair Advocate, offered on my website*), but I wanted to share *all* of it. The information has really helped me, and I am hoping it will help you as well. This revised regimen builds on the information provided in the first book, which I like to think of now as the ***beginner's edition*** because I was just starting to get a clue about hair care. I like to think of this book as the ***intermediate***, and probably **final**, ***edition***. Because taking care of our hair is an evolving process, and we are constantly learning, I am reluctant to ever say that my knowledge is advanced or that I am an expert. However, I do think I have uncovered enough new information to finally warrant a second edition. I hope you agree after reading it…

For those of you who may already be following the Six-Week regimen from the first book, you don't have to worry that I am completely throwing it out of the window. In fact, far from it – I am just *tweaking* and *enhancing* the foundation of the original regimen, which will mean fewer products to buy and a more flexible regimen that supports our busy schedules with routines for swimmers and ladies who workout. When I wrote the first book, I was just so excited to have my hair looking healthy and noticeably growing *for once* that I realize now that I got carried away in letting ladies know ALL the products I had tried or was using. Even though I did indicate on the shopping lists, which items were *required, suggested*, or *optional*, I have learned that some ladies still **bought everything**, even the items described as *optional*! It was not my goal to make anyone spend a mint. *I was just trying to give choices.* This time I am providing a significantly shortened product list, and I will try to help readers narrow down selections by suggesting that you **pick one or two** products from the various lists. I know that won't prevent many of us from being undercover product junkies, but at least you won't be able to blame it all on me!

As I work toward reaching my hair goals and witness other women in search of their own, it has become obvious that the secret to achieving beautiful, healthy hair is not in any one particular product or treatment. It is also often not the same answer for everyone, but the common thread appears to be a lifestyle of consistent hair care where you value your hair and make time to give it the best treatment you can. Commitment and consistency – doing "what you know to do" for, or to, your hair on a daily basis. Unfortunately, the doing "what you know to do" part is what used to be unclear to me, as I am sure it is for a lot of women. This is why I formulated the hair care regimen you are about to read, hopefully making it easier for you to find out what works for you. This regimen in a nutshell is me taking years of advice I have heard and read from various stylists, hair care experts and hair role models, as well as my mistakes and the experiences I have had along the way. I know it can look complicated in print, but it is really very easy to follow once you get started. I'll admit that a lot of it is commonsense information, but it is written in **great** detail so there is no guesswork as to what I am doing to get my results. Also, in anticipating potential questions, I would rather give too much information rather than too little.

Using quality products like the ones I am about to share, or those of your own choosing, in the regimen's framework should help to improve the overall condition of your hair, as well as increase length, when consistently followed. This is exactly what happened to my hair! Since I have been following this regimen, my hair went from just touching my shoulders to touching the bottom of my bra strap (only when it's straight), which in itself was a dream come true for me.

This is me in the 90's *before* the regimen.

This is how my hair looked *after* in July 2003.

I'll admit that reaching this goal, with healthy-looking ends, was not easy for me. Regardless, I am pleased to be making progress again as I have had a few setbacks over the past two years – thinning caused by overprocessing, dryness and breakage due in part to chronic anemia and poor diet, and a loss of 2-3 inches after a visit to a scissor-happy stylist. So I feel really good about the results I am achieving as I follow this new and improved regimen. I have even set a new goal, I would love to have bra-strap length hair (when it is curly) – a goal I hope to reach by my 40th birthday. A girl can dream, can't she? Only time will tell, but I feel good about this revised regimen, and I have found it gives us greater flexibility on how we use the recommended products to minimize or correct hair ailments such as split-ends, dryness, breakage and slow growth. It also gives us strategies for maintaining our hair as we become more active (e.g., swimming, working out, etc.).

It is my hope that this guide will give you the information and tips you need to make a major change in the way you care for your hair and in the way it looks! With the recommendations on products and techniques, as well as expert-recommended treatments (e.g., hot oil, protein, reconstructors, etc.) provided in this book, you should be on the road to beautiful, healthier hair, literally in six weeks! Many of the ladies who have written me regarding the first book said this was the case for them. So I truly hope this new and improved regimen will bring even better results for us, and help longer, healthier hair become the norm for black women, *not the exception*. So with that said, let's get started on our journey...

Chapter 2

GETTING STARTED

As before, the foundation for my Six-Week Regimen begins with a *consistent* shampooing and conditioning regimen. This should be true for whatever hair care regimen you practice. Have you ever noticed that the longer you go without shampooing your hair, the harder it becomes to keep it shiny and soft? When I was in college I would go for weeks without shampooing my hair, and I remember putting Luster's Pink lotion on it thinking that would help "fix" it. Putting this lotion on my dirty hair did not *fix* anything. All it did was make my dry hair sticky and hard. After reading all of the wonderful claims on the Pink lotion's bottle (e.g., moisturizes, helps prevent split-ends, etc.), I blamed "the product" for my dry, split-end filled hair. Now after maturing a bit, I realize I cannot blame any product for my bad hair days in college. **I was to blame. It was *my* fault.** However, it usually feels better to blame a stylist or product (*I blamed both for a lot of years*), but sometimes we have to admit when it is our fault. So I will admit now that for many years: **I** *did not shampoo/condition my hair on a regular basis;* **I** *never deep conditioned my hair;* **I** *used a blow dryer whenever I shampooed;* **I** *used a curling iron or electric curlers every time I styled my hair (sometimes twice a day);* **I** *used lots of holding spray, mousse and other alcohol-laden styling products;* **I** *combed/brushed roughly and frequently;* and **I** *slept on cotton pillow cases without any type of protection for my hair.* **I did all of those things**, so I cannot blame any stylist or product for the condition my hair was in for many years. I truly did not know any better at the time, and you can only do what you know to do, right?.

Finding A Regimen That Works

So, like many other women, I found myself going from product to product, stylist to stylist, thinking that I would find some magic solution to cure my hair ills. I did not realize until a few years ago that the real *solution* does not lie in any one stylist (*unless they take care of your hair on a daily basis*) or product – the real solution to our hair ills lies in a comprehensive hair care regimen that *we* control. Stylists can only make suggestions, offer advice, and style or treat our hair, but ultimately ***we are in the driver's seat*** when it comes to what happens to our hair on a daily, weekly or monthly basis – this is *our regimen*. Webster defines "regimen" as *a systematic course of treatment or training*, and "systematic" can be defined as a *regular method or order*. So what I am saying in a nutshell is that to have healthy hair we need our own personalized *treatment/training for our hair that we follow according to a regular method or order*, not just doing *whatever, whenever* and *however* we feel like it.

As I started to build my regimen, the first and most important lesson I learned is that *our hair,* regardless of its type (oily, normal, dry, etc.) should be shampooed **at least** *once a week*. However, as I have learned more recently, for many of us, shampooing twice a week (i.e., every 3-4 days) is necessary to maintain the proper moisture balance and keep our scalp healthy and free from product build-up. Although some people with dry hair or scalp conditions may be wary of actually using shampoo this often, there are ways to protect our hair from the harsh effects of many popular shampoos. I list the ones I am familiar with in this chapter (e.g., only lathering once, adding oil to your shampoo, doing cleansing rinses with conditioners, etc.). *As always, you do have choices.* You can follow the example regimen I share with you in Chapter 3, or you can let your hair *or* doctor's orders be your guide (Ex. If you have certain skin or scalp conditions/diseases, a doctor may make a recommendation on shampooing – products and frequency, etc.).

The Importance of Shampooing & Conditioning

In the first edition of this book, I used to shampoo my hair once a week. However, as my hair situation changed, and I experienced excessive dryness, which could have been caused by bouts with anemia, my diet, use of the Pill or a dry house – I don't know the sole culprit, but I had to *let my hair be my guide.* This led me to start shampooing every 3-4 days. Before adopting this revised regimen, my hair became *very* dry and felt like straw by the fourth or fifth day after a shampoo, and the dryness got worse with each day that passed. It was also easily tangled and difficult to comb. No matter how many oils or moisturizers I apply to my hair when it is like this, the feel and texture of it *will not* change until I shampoo or wet it, and it does not matter if I am in week 1 or week 12 of a relaxer. Just like skin, our hair needs to be hydrated on a regular basis, and no product can replace regular hydration. By ignoring my hair's *changed* need and dehydration for over a year, I suffered needless dryness and experienced unnecessary breakage. *Dry, dehydrated hair tends to break…*

Shampooing our hair not only cleanses it, but it also replenishes much needed moisture. Unlike our sisters of other ethnicities, our hair gets drier each week that it is not shampooed, *not oilier*. First the texture of the hair changes, and then the hair becomes vulnerable and prone to breakage. I know some of us still believe that **not** shampooing our hair on a regular basis is okay. I have even heard some of us say that dirty hair curls better (*I used to think this*). However, contrary to that belief, clean hair not only curls better, it is also better able to withstand the normal wear and tear of day-to-day styling, without excessive breakage. I must also add that, although clean hair is good, *clean, well-conditioned hair is better*. Your hair cannot *successfully* withstand regular chemical treatments, heat styling and normal, daily wear and tear without being properly conditioned. So any regimen you follow must include consistent shampooing *and* conditioning.

The way you shampoo and condition (e.g., products used, frequency, etc.) your hair plays a more critical role in your hair's overall health than the stylist you go to or the chemicals you have applied (e.g., texturizers, relaxers, color, etc.). The shampoo, conditioner, leave-ins and moisturizers you use on your hair in your daily/weekly regimen can make the biggest difference in how healthy your hair looks, how much length you are able to sustain and how long chemical treatments look fresh. By consistently following my Six-Week Regimen, outlined in Chapter 3, my hair still looks good even when I am in need of a touch-up (when there is significant new growth, I used to wait every 5-6 weeks, but now I am able to make it to at least 12 weeks).

Developing Your Own Regimen

As you read my personalized regimen in the next few chapters, please note that *the recommendations and tips included are only suggestions.* **I am not saying that there is only one route to healthy hair** because *every woman's hair is different*, with unique problems and needs. However, I am providing the steps that I follow in my quest to take better care of my hair and to achieve significant growth. Just as you might ask a lady in the mall what she does to get her hair the way it is (*I have done this*), once she tells you, you can either accept it and use the information as given, tweak it, or disregard it completely. You may notice that I am writing this book as if we are having a conversation – the only difference is that I am answering questions that I have gotten from many different women over the years, and the information is presented in **great** detail. So with that said, if the steps outlined in this book are not perfectly suited to your hair type or lifestyle, you can treat my regimen as a foundation to create your own personalized regimen. **I am not a licensed hair professional,** and I do not claim to have the best plan for every person's hair. However, I do believe that the information contained in this book can help improve the condition of the average black woman's hair – whether it is relaxed or natural, long or short.

First Step – A Hair Assessment

Before you read through my regimen and work to come up with your own personalized regimen, you should take a good look at your overall hair care habits over the last few years and your current hair situation. You may need to discuss your assessments or concerns with a stylist, cosmetologist or dermatologist, and if a problem is identified, it should be addressed or corrected before you can expect to reap the full benefit from any new regimen, *regardless of how good it is.* Are you coloring or relaxing your own hair, yet *you have not been trained to do so?* Relaxing more than once every 6-8 weeks? Frequently wearing tight braids, weaves or wigs for extended periods of time? Hot curling every day? Combing/brushing roughly? Not having split-ends trimmed? Is any of this you? If it is, and you are experiencing problems (e.g., bald spots, receding hair lines, thinning, breakage, excessive shedding, etc.), you must **first** try to stabilize whatever hair situation you may have going on, and try to stop it from going any further. *In other words, you want to keep a bad situation from getting worse.* To give you an example, if you are relaxing every three to four weeks, hot curling every day and/or walking around with a head full of split-ends, a good first step would be to have any split or damaged ends trimmed by a trusted stylist. However, don't confuse *trimming* damaged or split-ends with cutting it all off or making it all one length. I know some stylists can go to the extreme, but the goal should be to start with healthy ends. Otherwise, you may not notice a significant improvement in your hair, even if you start following the best regimen in the world. So to make sure that you are getting off to a good, fresh start, *fix whatever obvious problems you can find first*. However, if you can't pinpoint the cause or source of certain conditions, a trip to your personal physician or dermatologist might be helpful.

Selecting Products & Going For It!

Once you handle the serious issues, then the next step is to find the best, *not necessarily most expensive*, products for your hair (I will make recommendations in Chapter 3, based on my experiences, to help with this task). From there, you must then come up with a routine that works for *you*, using the products that work for you on a consistent basis (I will also give you an example of a regimen that I follow in Chapter 3). As you follow **your** new or revised regimen, you may need to tweak it periodically to meet your changing hair needs, but regardless of how it changes, *your regimen* must become a lifelong endeavor *if* you expect to *continue* getting good results. Just like taking care of our bodies, skin and teeth have become a way of life, so must taking care of our hair… The hair care regimen you are about to build (or revise) must become a way of life if you hope to have the beautiful, healthier hair you have always dreamed of.

So with all of this said, I would like to offer a *few* (few is such a relative term) tips that are not only helpful for the *Six-Week Regimen*, but also for any hair care regimen you follow.

Shampooing & Conditioning Tips

1. **Read the "Back" Labels**, mainly the ingredients, when you select products for your hair. I used to only read the front or the benefits – I never really cared what was **in** the product. Now, having a little more experience after years of trying to diagnose causes of dryness, I started to find surprise ingredients in products that I thought were "good" for my hair. As an example, in my first book and on my website, I mentioned that Keragenics Revitalizing Protein Pac was a good alternative to the Rx Prescriptions Protein Pac I used to use,

but in comparing the two product's ingredient lists, I realize this may not have been the wisest choice. For some reason, the Keragenics product not only has cetyl alcohol, but it also has sodium lauryl sulfate – WHY???? As I have learned over the last couple of years, this is a pretty harsh cleansing agent found in many popular shampoos – why is it in a protein conditioner? I cannot even begin to understand why, and since my hair tends to be dry, I first switched back to the Rx Prescriptions Protein Pac and then, later, to a natural product. I have purposely switched from shampoos containing this ingredient, so I surely don't want it in my conditioner. **Bottom line** … **read the labels** *before* **buying**.

2. Be careful when using hair care products that claim to work for **all** hair types – some do, but many don't (e.g., Head & Shoulders, etc.). I am especially suspicious of shampoos and conditioners that make this claim. Our hair usually gets drier with each day that passes; whereas, the hair of women of other ethnicities often tends to get oilier – so how can the same shampoo sufficiently add the moisture we need as well as remove excess oils from oilier types? Also, many of the conditioners designed with white women in mind usually don't contain as many oils or moisturizers as the average black woman might need in hers. Some of these products can be a little too drying for our hair – even so-called baby shampoos that usually have cute white kids on the bottle tend to be too drying for my sons' hair and even for many black women. So in your product searches, read labels and look at pictures on the products, if applicable, to make sure that the products you select are designed with your particular hair type (e.g., dry, damaged, color-treated, relaxed, etc.) in mind. If they don't say, and you are in doubt, **you may want to try a different product** that specifically mentions your hair type *unless* the product in question is highly recommended by a trusted stylist or someone that you know with a similar hair type.

3. Don't assume that expensive hair care products are always better than less expensive ones. I have tried expensive, as well as inexpensive products, and I can honestly say that the cost of the products used does not determine the success of your hair care regimen or how good your hair looks. In fact, over the last few years, I have uncovered shampoos, conditioners, and treatments that give salon results, that are *relatively* cheap. Surprisingly, most of the products I recommend can be found in your local beauty supply store, salon or in various online stores.

4. Select products that are specified for home use. Try to avoid "professional use only" products. Of course, there are always exceptions, but this is really important if you perm or color your own hair.

5. When selecting shampoos and conditioners look for products containing ingredients such as jojoba, rosemary, chamomile, olive oil and other herbal extracts, as well as vitamin E.

6. When selecting a shampoo, you *may* want to avoid products that contain harsh detergents like sodium lauryl sulfate. Although there are many women who find success with shampoos that contain this ingredient, for those of you who may be concerned, sodium **laureth** sulfate and ammonium laureth sulfate are supposed to be *somewhat* gentler sudsing agents. However, if you have problems with dryness or scalp irritation, you may want to avoid them all together by switching to natural products or ones that don't contain these agents. If you are ever analyzing your regimen to see what area could be giving you a problem, you may want to check out the labels on your favorite shampoos, and believe it or not, conditioners too. If there is a problem, don't be afraid to switch products. There is never a shortage of products to choose from, believe me, I KNOW!

7. If you really like or don't want to throw away a shampoo(s) that contain ingredients like sodium lauryl sulfate, you could make yours a little less harsh with a few at-home tweaks. You could add a few drops of oils such as almond, coconut, rosehip or jojoba to a capful of shampoo before applying it to make sure that your hair is clean, but not stripped of its natural oils. You can also dilute the shampoo with a small amount of distilled water, aloe juice or aloe gel. However, just in case you don't like the final outcome (e.g., too watery,

too oily, no longer lathers, etc.), mix whatever you add to the shampoo in its cap or a mixing cup (you can use a bobby pin or a toothpick), *not in the bottle unless it is almost gone. Some shampoos are too expensive to make a mistake that you can't correct.*

8. Even if your shampoo does not contain any of the harsh chemicals mentioned above, many can still be drying. Even natural shampoos contain some form of soap, which can still cause dryness in some women. So to further reduce the risk of dryness, you can also add a few drops of natural oils (e.g., almond, coconut, jojoba, rosehip, etc.) to your favorite shampoo or any of the ones mentioned in the Six-Week Regimen. You can even dilute them with a small amount of distilled water, aloe juice or gel. Again, do your mixing in the cap or a mixing cup.

9. Honey is said to be a natural humectant. I have also heard of people adding a small amount of honey to their shampoo to add body and volume. I did it once, and I did see some benefit, but I was too lazy to continue using it – it was just too sticky. However, for those wanting to experiment, I am just throwing it out there. Just remember to mix it in the cap or a mixing cup – I don't want you to accidentally ruin a good bottle of shampoo.

10. I remember watching commercials when I was a kid that showed white women in the shower lathering their hair with suds galore, rubbing the shampoo everywhere, just having a good old time. Then afterwards, you would always see them with their shiny, healthy-looking hair bouncing around. This looked so good to me that it made me think the more suds and the more rubbing you do during a shampoo, the better. *I don't know about for them, but for us, this is definitely not true!* Because many shampoos today contain strong cleansing agents (e.g., sodium lauryl sulfate, etc.), unless our hair is extremely dirty or we are shampooing out chemicals, we should try to limit our shampooing to just **one** lather. This can be done by rinsing the hair thoroughly for a few minutes **before** applying a small amount of shampoo to a few sections of our hair and scalp (e.g., left front, back right, etc.) – parting it down the middle helps. To help with this I have a cap full of shampoo that I dole out in fourths. I only use more shampoo if I really, really need it. The rule is to use only as much shampoo you need to clean your scalp – you truly don't need that big white lather that extends from your scalp all the way to the top of your ends. If you are careful, a little truly goes a long way.

11. Make sure you shampoo your hair whenever it feels dirty, sticky, overly dry and difficult to moisturize or has been exposed to chlorine. Dirty hair is harder to curl, often requiring extra heat, and is more susceptible to breakage and heat damage. For those of you wearing braids/extensions, an itchy scalp might be another indicator. I know many ladies wearing braids try to preserve their braid styles by cleansing the scalp with cotton balls soaked with Sea Breeze or Witch Hazel instead of shampooing. This may buy you some additional time, but at some point actual shampooing will be needed. You can consult your braider for advice if you are not sure, or consult a book like <u>Plaited Glory For Colored Girls Who've Considered Braids, Locks, And Twists</u> by Lonnice Breittenum Bonner. I have heard that it offers a lot of practical tips on handling different types of braids during the shampooing and conditioning process. I admit that I am not an expert in braids, but I think you should shampoo whenever your hair is suffering from the symptoms described above.

12. I have heard and read recommendations that braids should only be shampooed once every two weeks, but depending on the braids, I think using a moisturizing shampoo weekly may be beneficial. I have heard that clear shampoos work best because they don't leave residue or flakes. Rinse thoroughly, and *gently* massage the shampoo into the scalp between the braids. Some recommend diluting the shampoo with distilled water before applying. Regardless of how you choose to do it, **make sure the entire length of each braid is cleansed and rinsed.** Even if you choose not to actually shampoo weekly, you could still rinse the hair or do a conditioning rinse, smoothing a crème conditioner on the braids and rinsing (see Chapter 3 for more details). I have heard braid wearers talk of shampooing their braids and extensions by placing a stocking cap

over them beforehand, which is said to reduce the risk of flyaway hair or frizz on the braids. *I am not sure how well this works*, but it is an option to consider. You can talk to your braider or other braid wearers for tips on successfully doing this.

13. Weaves and extensions must be shampooed regularly as well, *while they are on your head or separately*. You can talk to the stylist who added the hair for the best ways to shampoo and condition to preserve your style. Either way, I am more concerned with the health of **your** hair and scalp. I know synthetic and human hair respond differently to shampoos and conditioners, but **your** hair and scalp need regular hydration, so be careful not to take any advice that jeopardizes the health of your own hair. I am talking about any advice that tells you to go weeks without hydrating your hair. Even if you just do conditioning rinses (see Chapter 3), you have to *wet* your hair and scalp on a regular basis to keep it clean and moist.

14. If you wear a wig, it is imperative that you keep your hair shampooed and conditioned at least once a week. Wearing wigs can be very drying to the hair and scalp, *even if you wear a stocking cap underneath*. As a result, your hair must be hydrated on a regular basis, even if it is just a cleansing rinse. The same advice goes for chemically-treated hair.

15. For your weekly shampoo, pick a convenient time when you have at least an hour to spare where you can shampoo, deep condition if necessary, as well as comb and detangle your hair without rushing (mid-week shampoos usually take less time, examples are described in Chapter 3). Your hair is most vulnerable when it is wet, so rough handling due to rushing can be a major cause of breakage. To avoid this, pick days where you don't have as much going on or where you can easily squeeze a shampoo in. As an example, pick a day where you know you are going to swim, or you have a little time to pamper yourself and your hair, or just fit it in at the same time you plan to shower.

16. The shampooing and conditioning regimen described in Chapter 3 is **not** meant to replace the shampooing/conditioning routine you would follow after applying a relaxer to your hair. I hope you are not doing it yourself, unless you are a trained stylist or cosmetologist, but if you are, ***shampoo and condition according to the directions provided by the manufacturer of the relaxer you are using.*** The Six-Week Regimen is for the shampoos that start days or weeks **after** your chemical treatments (e.g., relaxer, texturizer, etc.).

17. If you suffer from scalp conditions such as dry scalp, dandruff or psoriasis, or your scalp has been burned or damaged, you may want to try Paul Mitchell's Tea Tree Special Shampoo or a shampoo that contains soothing herbs or oils like tea tree or aloe. My stylist used the Paul Mitchell product on my hair once when my scalp was burned during a touch-up, and it was the most refreshing shampoo my scalp has ever had. My scalp literally tingled. If it alleviates or corrects your scalp condition, you may want to substitute (periodically or permanently) it for the shampoo specified in the *Six-Week Regimen* (or your regular shampoo).

18. If you suffer from a dry scalp condition, your hair and/or scalp might benefit from a pre-shampoo treatment of Healthier Hair in a Bottle! Oil Spray (visit www.blackwomansguide.com or you could substitute some other natural oil, like warm olive oil). Massage the oil into the scalp and hair the night before you shampoo, or, at a minimum, 30 minutes before. This can also be done for women with a normal scalp to keep it healthy and to reduce the drying effects of shampoos.

19. If your ends tend to be really dry, in addition to not putting any shampoo directly on them, you could put a small amount of crème conditioner on the bottom three inches of the hair (from the ends up) **before shampooing** to protect them. Then shampoo as normal, avoiding your ends as much as possible. You could

also do a more intensive pre-shampoo conditioning routine by putting your favorite crème conditioner on all of your hair (not scalp) for however long you have to spare before shampooing (e.g., 10 minutes, 15 minutes, etc.).

20. Another dry hair treatment is to apply Aveda Sap Moss Nourishing Concentrate Pre-Shampoo Healing Treatment for Dry Hair to damp hair for 1-2 minutes (I have kept it on longer) before shampooing. This stuff is expensive, but it is great! It is only sold at Aveda Concept stores (see www.aveda.com). The bottle says that it can be used every five shampoos (once or twice a month, depending on your routine), so it should last a while. I have also found that this product works very well for me as I try to make it to the 12th week in my relaxer – it definitely helps soften new growth. See the Severely Dry Hair Treatment section in Chapter 3.

21. Before shampooing, clip or file any jagged or split fingernails that might snag your hair. There have been times during my shampoos where I have had at least one fingernail that gets caught on a strand of hair, and the strand usually breaks. So to avoid unnecessary breakage, check out your nails before each shampoo.

22. Start every shampoo off by rinsing your hair thoroughly with warm water (a few minutes or seconds, depending on your water pressure, hair texture, etc.). The more you rinse, the easier it is to create a lather and the less shampoo you will need to get your hair clean – this saves money and minimizes the drying effects of shampoo. If you'd like, you could also try KeraCare's 1st Lather Shampoo first to remove excess oils and product build-up, then do your actual shampoo. One of my cousins uses this on her hair and her daughter's hair with really good results.

23. Realize that there are different focuses for shampooing vs. conditioning. During your shampoo, you should focus on cleansing the **scalp,** not the hair and ends, trying not to rub the hair excessively. As the hair is rinsed, the shampoo that runs down the hair shaft is *usually* sufficient to clean it, unless you are trying to remove chlorine or some other chemical. If not, applying shampoo directly to the ends wastes shampoo and causes unnecessary drying. On the other hand, conditioning should focus on the **hair and ends,** *especially the ends* – these areas are often in need of the most care. Putting creme conditioners on the scalp can cause build-up, flaking and itching. Hot oil treatments (ones that don't contain mineral oil or petroleum) would be the exception, which are for the hair and scalp.

24. When shampooing your hair, gently massage the scalp with your fingertips – do not use your fingernails! Even if you have flakes or build-up on your scalp, just massage it away with your fingertips. Many women, especially stylists, use their fingernails when shampooing hair. Not only is this unnecessary, it may also damage your scalp – *regardless of how good it feels at the time!*

25. When you shampoo or rinse, keep your hair in a straight back position *if you can* (usually accomplished by shampooing in the shower or a stylist's chair) and massage the scalp without vigorously rubbing the hair. A lot of scrubbing and rubbing of the hair in different directions causes hair to tangle and mat – no one needs this, especially ladies with natural hair. Keeping the hair in the direction it normally falls, while it is wet, can help to prevent tangling and matting, especially if you have braids, extensions or a weave. With my relaxed hair I noticed that flipping it forward in the sink or tub to rinse out a conditioner and putting it up high on my head with a towel causes me unnecessary tangling. As a result, I now try to rinse out my hair in the shower or turned to the side in the sink or tub, and then gently use the towel to remove excess moisture as the hair hangs, instead of putting the hair up high on my head. The more tangling we can avoid, the less breakage we should experience.

26. Some ladies with really dry hair may benefit from a mid-week shampoo. See the Mid-Week/Refresher Shampoo section, which follows Week 6 of the regimen in Chapter 3 for a suggested routine/regimen.

28. Some ladies have started replacing their regular shampoo with a *shampoo-less* washing/cleansing, where shampoo is replaced by a conditioner. Although I have heard a few people rave about it (it is said to be less drying than regular shampooing), I did not find it cleansing enough to replace my weekly shampoo. However, I mention it because *everyone is different*, and if you find you need to tweak the suggested shampooing and conditioning regimen I describe in Chapter 3, this might be something new to try. I also mention a similar *mini-regimen* in the same chapter (under the Work-out/Mid-Week Conditioning Rinse section) that I use after working out or before a touch-up.

29. Regardless of how you decide to shampoo or how often, whenever you do would also be a good time to clean your combs and brushes. You can do this by throwing them into the sink or shower as you shampoo. Then rinse them out as you rinse your hair. Keeping my combs and brushes clean is something I struggle to remember, so this is definitely a tip that I am trying to incorporate into my own routine. Re-using dirty hair appliances can get our clean hair dirty faster, so we do need to keep these items clean.

30. Don't believe the claims of products that combine a shampoo and conditioner and promise the same results of shampooing and conditioning the hair separately. When I was younger I loved the idea of saving time and effort by eliminating the conditioning step. I always washed my hair in the shower so the thought of a one-step shampoo and conditioner was very appealing. However, after years of not getting the results that I wanted, a stylist I visited in college told me that *our* hair should always be conditioned separately, especially if it has been chemically-treated. Despite its coarse nature, our hair has special conditioning needs – it needs to be moisturized as well as strengthened. To maximize the benefits of your conditioner, you can use heat or *deep condition* (with a heating cap, dryer or hot towel) as needed, *unless the conditioner specifically recommends that it not be used with heat.*

31. If your hair is damaged from overprocessing or you are experiencing breakage and excessive shedding, you might want to try Aphogee's Treatment for Damaged Hair (the one that makes your hair hard). I have tried it a number of times with mixed results, but there are people who swear by it, namely my stylist. I have heard some even say that it has helped them stretch the time between relaxers. I plan to try it again, but in the meantime, I decided to mention it here in case some of you might want to try it. If you try it, **be sure to follow the directions carefully**. Because this is a heavy-duty protein treatment, the deep conditioning step (sitting under a dryer/heating cap with the Aphogee Balancing Moisturizer or a similar crème conditioner) is *very* important. In addition to that, it might also be helpful to go easy on leave-in treatments that contain protein (e.g., Infusium 23, ApHOGEE Keratin & Green Tea Restructurizer, etc.) afterwards to reduce the risk of your hair feeling dry or brittle.

32. When you deep condition your hair, warm olive oil can be used with your normal conditioner or with the crème conditioners recommended in the *Six-Week Regimen*. It could also be used instead of the hot-oil treatment in Week 2.

33. As I said earlier, do not put crème conditioners on your scalp. I used to do this with conditioners like Aphogee Balancing Moisturizer, and the result was usually white build-up on my scalp that I had to shampoo out. *Being dense, it took me a while to realize what was causing it.* As with any rule, there are exceptions, KeraCare Dry & Itchy Scalp conditioner is supposed to be massaged into your hair and scalp. *Again*, my cousin has tried this and says that it is very good. Although I only experience itchy scalp symptoms on rare occasions, this is on the top of my list of new products to try. **Bottom line:** Unless a crème conditioner's label says it should be applied to the scalp, you *shouldn't put it there*, but even it does, if you start having problems with build-up on your scalp, stop doing it.

34. Some people like to comb crème conditioner through their hair before rinsing it out to minimize tangling during the post-rinse comb-through. However, I don't do this because in most cases you will still have to

comb your hair again after you rinse, and I think that the extra combing of wet hair could result in unnecessary breakage. Instead, I just separate my hair into 4 or 5 sections, and smooth the conditioner gently from roots to ends, *avoiding the scalp*. I then rinse, detangle, and gently comb through as needed.

34. If you find that your hair is pretty healthy and you are using pretty decent products consistently, but you experience excessive tangling after rinsing your conditioner out, it *may* not be your hair or the products you are using. Sometimes, the problem could lie in your water. Many areas have "hard" water or water that has trace amounts of chemicals or elements (e.g., iron, lead, chlorine, etc.) that can be left behind on your hair, making it feel dry or tangled. This is also common where people might have well water and their filtration systems do not remove all of the sediment or minerals from it. If you think this could be the case in your area, you might consider buying a jug of distilled water that you can use for your final rinse after conditioning your hair. Also, Ion makes a Hard Water Conditioner that works pretty well, especially after you've been swimming in a chlorinated pool. You can use it as you would your normal conditioner, or it can be used beforehand as protection from the chlorine.

35. Again, if you experience excessive tangling after shampooing and conditioning, but you don't think it is the water, you may want to try an acidifying conditioner like Nexus Ensure Acidifying Conditioner & Detangler, which helps promote smooth and tangle-free hair, while restoring the natural pH. Although these are claims of the manufacturer, I must say my hair was relatively tangle-free, even after swimming. This product is not all-natural by any means, but it does contain herbal, fruit and plant extracts, including aloe. It can be found at stores carrying Nexus products. For more information, try www.nexxus.com or call 1-800-444-NEXXUS. Other good detangling conditioners include: Roux Porosity Control pH 4.5 Corrector & Conditioner and KeraCare Humecto Crème Conditioner.

36. If your hair has been damaged, tends to be very dry or is recovering from past abuse, you may need to do a weekly deep conditioning treatment (sitting under a heating cap/dryer) where you stay under the dryer for 15-30 minutes, if possible. When I wrote the first edition of this book, I used to sit under my dryer or heating cap for at least 30 minutes every time I deep conditioned, and I was able to get my hair back to a healthy state in a relatively short amount of time. However, as years passed, I got a little lazy and rushed and started only doing it for 10 minutes or less. Shortly thereafter, I started to notice a little more dryness than usual. Because this was not the only area where I was slipping, *it is hard to say that this is definitely the reason, but I know that it was at least a small part of it*. As a result, if there is a time when you are not getting the results you want in your regimen, this could be an area to consider as you are troubleshooting.

37. Even if you choose not to follow the *Six-Week Regimen* completely, remember to deep condition your hair at least twice a month (*mention this to your stylist if you go to the salon for shampoos*). Make that *4 times* a month if your hair has been subjected to frequent heat styling and/or you are trying to get it to a healthier state. 15 to 30 minutes under a heating cap or dryer should do it, depending on the condition and texture of your hair. *Fine hair or hair that is not chemically-treated, damaged or subjected to frequent heat styling may require less time under the dryer, if any at all*. However, if you do decide to deep condition, *please be sure to follow ALL of the manufacturer's instructions for your heating cap or dryer*. There may be special warnings for people with certain illnesses or conditions (e.g., diabetes, circulatory problems, etc.). Before sitting under the heating cap or dryer, find a task that you want to accomplish or work towards during this time. As an example, you could give yourself a manicure or a pedicure, read, clip coupons, make to-do lists, daydream, relax or write a book, *like I did*. Link this treatment with accomplishing goals, and the investment of time may not seem so large. The results you get will far outweigh any perceived time loss.

38. If for some reason you cannot sit under a dryer or a heating cap, or you choose not to, as an alternative, you could also wear an oil-based conditioner on your hair overnight. I have yet to try this, but I have heard of

women who do and get really good results. After shampooing and rinsing, you could apply the conditioner of your choice (e.g., olive oil or a hot oil treatment of your choice like Healthier Hair in a Bottle! Hot Oil Treatment), and cover your hair with a plastic shower or processing cap. Put a towel on your pillow, and sleep on it overnight. Rinse it out in the morning, and continue with the next step in your regimen.

39. If you decide not to apply heat with your conditioner, it becomes very important that you squeeze out excess water **before** applying your conditioner. Excess water can dilute conditioners, so if you want to maximize on the conditioning benefits you receive, make sure your hair is not sopping wet. You can also lightly towel it dry, but don't do any intensive wringing of your hair. While the conditioner is on you can pull your hair back or pin it up. From there, you could finish your shower, shave, take a bubble bath, or you could go about your normal activities around the house with the conditioner in your hair (*wearing a thin plastic cap would be a good idea*) before rinsing it out. This might be a good approach for little girls who don't want to/can't sit under a dryer. My cousin was telling me that she shampoos her daughter's hair near bath time (say after swimming) and leaves the conditioner on while she takes her bath. Afterwards, she rinses it out. Even though her hair is relaxed, and she swims a bit, this provides a good amount of conditioning for her. Maybe it can for you or your daughter too.

40. An especially good time to treat your hair to a deep conditioning treatment is the week **before** applying chemicals to your hair such as relaxers and semi/permanent hair coloring. See Week 6 in the *Six-Week Regimen* for suggestions, but just because I point you to Week 6, doesn't mean that I am recommending that you get a touch-up at that time, *because I am not!* This week in the regimen just provides a really good treatment that prepares our hair to withstand chemical applications without being as likely to suffer damage or "shed in the bowl", and it should straighten quicker as well as accept color more readily.

41. After rinsing out your conditioner, take a look at your scalp to make sure there is no white residue left behind. Sometimes, small amounts of pre-shampoo treatments or conditioners can remain on your scalp, but it is important to remove them. I usually glance at my scalp in the mirror before applying leave-in treatments. If I see any white residue on my scalp, I massage the areas with my fingers and warm water until it is gone. Who wants to go through all the trouble to have clean, well-conditioned hair, only to have an itchy scalp? I know I don't! If the scalp is all clear, then proceed with the next step in your regimen.

42. To seal the cuticle of your hair, giving it a smoother look and feel, do your final rinse with cool water (as cool as you can stand) from the shower, tub or sink after conditioning your hair. Some ladies like to do different types of rinses instead, which I mention in the next few tips, but to get the job done, cool tap water works in most cases.

43. I have heard a lot of talk about ACV (apple cider vinegar) rinses over the past couple of years from women who swear by them to books that talk about all the wonders of apple cider vinegar, which is supposed to restore hair's acidity and add shine to it. You would do this as your final rinse (after shampooing or conditioning, depending on your regimen). The theory is that relaxers cause our hair to be too alkaline, and the ACV rinse supposedly helps make it more pH balanced. After hearing about this, I became very excited, and I tried a number of recipes from different sources. Unfortunately, each time I tried one, I hated the apple cider smell, my hair did not feel silky smooth like it normally did after I did my final rinse, and my ends seemed a little frizzier. This is what happened each time I tried one*, regardless of the recipe* I used *(one example was 3 parts water and 1 part apple cider vinegar – I even tried adding aloe, distilled water and green tea at different points).* So, I can't speak for your hair, but as for me, *until I see/hear something different*, I only like vinegar on my collard greens! This is why you won't see me recommending an ACV rinse in this book. However, if you want more information on ACV rinses, you can check out books on aromatherapy and herbs from your local library. You could also search the web, or post a question about

them on one of the many boards on the internet dedicated to black hair care (Yahoo has a large number of them).

44. Although I mentioned doing a final rinse with distilled water for those who might have hard water, this type of rinse can benefit you regardless of your water type. You can do a final rinse with just cool distilled water, or you can add or use rosewater and/or aloe juice separately. Both can be purchased from health food stores pretty cheaply and can be mixed with other ingredients of your choosing. Healthier Hair in a Bottle! Moisturizing & Detangling Mist (visit www.blackwomansguide.com) contains a number of these ingredients along with other natural moisturizing items, making it a great after-rinse detangler or light daily moisture boost for natural and relaxed hair, especially when curly styles are worn.

45. If your hair is coarse or is very tangled after shampooing and conditioning, you will want to handle it **very delicately** as you detangle and comb it with a very wide-tooth comb. I think the key for a successful comb-out is clean, well-conditioned hair that is *still wet*. One or more detangling leave-in conditioners would also be helpful. I recommend a number of them for you to choose from in Chapter 3, but some of the best products I have used more recently for detangling have been wrapping and setting lotions (e.g., Salon Finish, Nu Expressions, etc.). It never occurred to me to use them for this purpose until my cousin mentioned that she does not have a problem detangling her wet hair. After she told me her secret, I thought about the fact that you usually don't notice stylists struggling as much to comb-through wet hair as people at home do, and it may be because many of them use wrapping or setting lotions, not the regular leave-in treatments we do. I think this could be one of the reasons why our hair looks better when they do it. The Salon Finish For Silky Hair Foam Wrap & Style Lotion and Nu Expressions Wrapping Lotion products say they can even be used for blow drying as well as roller setting, which makes me think they could helpful for natural hair, *but I can't say how effective they will be*. All I can say is that products like these make detangling and air drying a whole lot easier for me, and they eliminated a lot of the leave-in treatments I used to use in my regimen. This tip alone could save many of us a lot of hair that might have been lost to unnecessary breakage.

46. Is your hair graying or already gray, and you have decided to stop coloring it? If so, *you do have options*. My cousin and I both have prematurely gray hair; however, I have chosen to fight it, but she has chosen to embrace it. If you choose to embrace it, like she has, you may want to try Shimmer Lights Original Conditioning Shampoo by Clairol Professional. Her stylist introduced her to it, and she confirms the manufacturer's claims that it "shampoos away yellow" and "leaves hair shiny without residue". She also told me about another product her stylist introduced her to, Fanci-Full Temporary Hair Color Rinse by Roux. In her case, she chose the formula for *highlighting* gray, and since she hipped me to it, I am using Formula 12 (Black Rage) to *cover* my gray. This product is more of a leave-in treatment than a rinse – it contains no ammonia or peroxide, the color is instantaneous and it seems to be non-damaging (as the manufacturer claims). It also contains a styling lotion, so I use it after every shampoo now. In addition to applying it with a nozzle bottle, I use cotton balls to work it through the stubborn gray around my edges and to catch any trickles that try to fall into my face. Even though I have had good experiences with this product, I strongly suggest that you *read and follow the directions on the bottle.* The product has worked well enough for me that I don't plan to use semi-permanent color again. So whether you are embracing or trying to hide your gray, you may want to consider one or more of these products. You can get more information on the rinse from www.rouxblue.com or by calling 1-800-933-4303.

47. If you tend to have dry, brittle hair or ends, it may be worth your while to read the labels of your leave-in treatments to determine if they contain protein (e.g., whey protein, keratin, etc.) and how much (you can tell by where the name appears in the ingredients list). This is especially important if you just did a protein conditioning treatment. While protein helps to strengthen our hair, for some of us, it can make it feel hard and brittle. If you ever tried Aphogee's Treatment for Damaged Hair, you may know what I am talking about.

Don't get me wrong, it is a good thing when you read these ingredients on a label, but make sure you don't use too many products containing protein at once (e.g., using a protein treatment, followed by leave-ins like Infusium 23 and Aphogee's Green Tea Restructurizing Treatment). You could wind up with well-conditioned hair that is very brittle, and **brittle hair is harder to comb**, which could mean unnecessary breakage. If this is the case for you, then using the leave-in treatments with protein could be too much of a good thing.

48. Make sure you don't brush your hair as you try to detangle it. You can gently brush it afterwards (e.g., smoothing down hair and edges as you air dry, etc.), but not while it is tangled – this is just breakage waiting to happen.

49. Another detangling option may be to use Luster's S-Curl "No Drip" Activator Moisturizer or similar activator sprays. I have heard women with natural hair say that these products can help make it easier to comb through their wet hair as they prepare to braid or twist it. I have also heard of some women using these products to help secure relaxed hair in a bun or if they are planning to braid or twist the wet hair. However, if you are trying to create a straight style (e.g., air drying, blow drying, etc.) activators may not be your best choice. It really depends on the style or look you are trying to create (e.g., braids, twists, etc.). If you do choose to try them, just remember that many activators contain a significant amount of glycerin, so you may not want to use them on your scalp because *they can cause itching for some women.*

50. Separating your hair into at least 4 sections and clipping the sections is a great way to manage wet hair, especially for ladies with natural hair and little girls. There should be a lot less pain and headache. For each section, use a wide-tooth comb for relaxed hair to detangle and comb. For natural hair, a wide-tooth pick might work better, but you can try either or both – *whichever works for you.* Keeping the hair wet definitely helps with the comb-out process. You can re-wet sections as they are drying by spraying distilled water, your favorite leave-in treatment or Healthier Hair in a Bottle! Moisturizing & Detangling Mist onto them as you are combing. *This is especially helpful for ladies with natural hair.* For my relaxed hair, I oil my scalp and hair with Healthier Hair in a Bottle! Oil Spray *after applying my leave-in treatments*, by parting small sections all over my head. I comb each section after I put oil on it. I do this when I am air drying or doing plait or twist sets. Ladies with natural hair can do this too, especially if you are going to braid or twist your wet hair.

51. After shampooing/conditioning/rinsing braids, be sure to gently towel dry the braids to remove excess moisture. Depending on the type of braids, you can lightly spray on a leave-in treatment and/or apply a little Healthier Hair in a Bottle! Oil Spray, which is easily sprayed on the scalp and smoothed on the braids. This will help seal in moisture and shine. Some braid wearers allow their braids to air dry out in the open or covered by a silk/satin scarf. Verify these recommendations with your braider if you have any questions or concerns.

52. If you choose to air dry relaxed hair using the Pony-tail Method described in Chapter 4, I mention using scrunchies or non-rubber elastic bands. However, I recently heard of a "Satin Center" scrunchie by *Hype Hair* that claims not to damage or pull hair. I haven't tried them yet, but they look like something definitely worth checking out as you can sometimes unnecessarily lose strands of hair when wearing scrunchies if you are not careful. I have been using the "Ouchless" Headbands by Goody (wrapped around about 4 times), which work very nicely.

53. If you blow dry your hair frequently (more than once a month), you might want to *try* Thermasilk products (shampoo and conditioner) by Helene Curtis. These products are *supposed* to be activated by heat, causing the hair's condition to improve as you blow dry or hot curl it. I am skeptical, but it is worth a try until you kick the blow drying habit (mainly an issue for ladies with relaxed hair). Until you do, please be careful using

the brush attachments and any other brush products claiming to automatically remove tangles from our hair (I am sure you have seen the ads over the past couple of years). I feel nervous just thinking about them – *it feels like breakage waiting to happen.*

54. If you can't see yourself living without a blow dryer, you might want to think about purchasing an ionic blow dryer. These blow dryers are "supposedly" (I don't know for sure) less damaging than the regular blow dryers and make claims to a number of different benefits. Ion, Conair and Revlon make versions of them. **I have not used them,** so read their claims, and you can be the judge.

55. In the next chapter you will have a chance to see the regimen I follow in taking care of my hair over 6 to 12 week periods. I know many of you may think I am crazy because I rotate at least 3 shampoos and at least 4 or 5 conditioners during that time! Is this necessary? Maybe not, but it is what works for me, and being the product junky that I am, I actually enjoy it. However, as you design your own regimen, if your hair is healthy and beautiful using the same shampoo every time and rotating only 1 or 2 conditioners, I say stick with it! Creating a regimen is all about finding what works for Y-O-U, not *me*. *So only rotate as many shampoos/conditioners as you feel you need to reach your hair goals.* If that means only 1 shampoo and 1 conditioner – if it works for you, go with that. Let *your* hair and budget be *your* guide.

56. Remember to continue your same shampooing and conditioning routine after you have a baby. If possible, keep the same stylist that took care of your hair during your pregnancy. Sometimes your hair may have special needs as the hormones associated with pregnancy leave your body and as you stop taking prenatal vitamins. My hair was surprisingly dry and brittle a few months after I had my first child, which was a major contrast to the soft, silky hair I sported during the pregnancy. To safeguard against unexpected changes in your hair's texture during this stressful time, make sure you continue to deep condition your hair even as you get busy with your new "mommy" role. To save time, dry your hair naturally (see Chapter 4). Also, try the overnight sets in Chapter 6 to help you still look your best during this hectic time. Finally, if you are breastfeeding, make sure you are getting enough water so that your hair is sufficiently hydrated.

I wanted to give you a *few* tips, but I know as usual, I got carried away! I hope I gave you a lot of good food for thought as well as many options that can be applied to your particular hair type and situation. Over the last few years, I have talked to so many people and heard so much interesting information that I wanted you all to benefit from it. As you may have noticed, all of the tips I just provided relate to shampooing, conditioning, rinsing, leave-in treatments, comb-outs and drying the hair. I also tried to throw in a few substitute or alternative products that can be used in conjunction with the *Six-Week Regimen* (Chapter 3) and *Drying Methods* (Chapter 4) sections. With all that said, I think you are more than ready to get started with the *Six-Week Regimen!*

Chapter 3

SIX-WEEK REGIMEN

Because of the coarse texture of my hair, I *used to* get a touch-up every 6 weeks, sometimes every 5. However, now that I have personally experienced the damaging effects relaxers can have on your hair when done too frequently (e.g., thinning/breakage around edges, dryness, brittleness, etc.), I now have one done every 12 to 14 weeks, which is my only appointment with a stylist. My old six-week relaxing schedule is what originally inspired me to develop my *Six-Week Regimen*. Even though I am waiting longer now, I still think the *Six-Week Regimen* applies for those of us who wait longer to relax **and** for those who have natural hair because we can just repeat the regimen continuously, adding variations here and there. My goal is to provide a structured framework, showing what I do, allowing readers to either follow it or devise their own regular shampooing and conditioning regimen. You can experiment at first to see if what works for me works for you, or try a few variations to find what works best. Once you find what works for you, *write it down* and *do it consistently throughout the year.* This is one of the best ways to actually see results in your hair – **find what works, and do it consistently**.

As you will find out later in this chapter, I shampoo my hair at least twice a week, about every 3-4 days. When I wrote the first edition of this book, I was just getting into shampooing once a week consistently, and once I saw the tremendous benefits and improvements in my hair, I started to do it faithfully. Although I would notice by the fifth or sixth day my hair wasn't looking as good as it did when I first shampooed it, I could still live with it until the next shampoo. At that point, once a week was all I could commit to, especially as I worked full-time and had two children under 3. Well, as I got older, and my hair started to gray more, by the fourth day into a shampoo, my hair was not as soft and shiny – it looked *dry* and *dull, regardless of whether it was freshly relaxed or not.* As I started trying to figure out what to do to correct this, I began to notice that on vacations, where I shampooed my hair at least 3 or 4 times a week after swimming, my hair looked so much better – even with the chlorine! My hair needed water – one shampoo a week was not enough to keep my hair soft and healthy-looking, regardless of my diet or how often I moisturized. This revelation caused me to tweak my old regimen and start following the *enhanced* regimen you are about to read in the following sections. This change in my regimen, combined with an improvement in my diet and vitamin intake along with more consistent moisturizing, put me back on the road to healthier, more beautiful hair, and I am hoping that will be the case for you too!

Please note that the regimen described in this chapter is a *home-based* hair care program that is designed for women who shampoo their hair at least once a week. For those who shampoo more than once a week, there are mini-shampooing/conditioning routines found later in this chapter that can be included for mid-week, post work-out and/or swimming. However, if you shampoo less than that (*most of us need to shampoo at least once a week* unless a trusted stylist or doctor has directed otherwise), you can still follow the regimen. Just pick up where you left off in the regimen the next time you shampoo (e.g., Week 1, Week 2, etc.). The weekly treatments included in this regimen are intended to help **Restore, Revitalize, Replenish, Repair, Rejuvenate** and **Resuscitate** your hair. Because you do something different each week for 6 weeks, you will experience different benefits each week.

The beauty of this regimen is that it allows you to "cross-train" your hair (if there *is* such a thing) by rotating shampoos and conditioners so that your hair does not become immune to the benefits of any of the products. I have heard stylists say that your hair can get *used to* a shampoo or conditioner if you use it too much. **I really don't know if this is true**, but I do think that using the same shampoo and conditioner repeatedly could cause the products to build up on our hair. However, there are many women who have beautiful hair using the same shampoo and conditioner week after week, year after year, so you never know. Regardless of your product selections, this regimen minimizes the risk of product "build-up" and eliminates the possibility of your hair becoming *immune* to any one shampoo or conditioner, *if such a thing exists*.

Even though I personally follow the steps in this regimen, they are only *suggestions*, and there is room for variation to accommodate your unique hair needs. You can obviously substitute products (some tips were provided in the previous chapter) and modify the regimen to suit your own personal hair care goals and preferences. Even so, for the first 6 weeks *if you do not already have a shampooing and conditioning regimen that you are happy with*, I do recommend that you try the steps in the regimen *as directed* to see if they work for you as well as they do for me. Then, if you would like to do some *fine-tuning* as you repeat the regimen, write your changes on the forms provided for each week's instructions. Also, if you should visit a hair salon to get your hair shampooed on a given week while you are following the *Six-Week Regimen*, just start where you left off in the regimen the next time you shampoo.

Shopping For Products

If you currently have a shampoo(s), conditioner(s) or leave-in treatment(s) that you like and are having success with, **you can postpone shopping if you would like to start the regimen off by substituting your favorites in for the products I suggest and/or use in my Six-Week regimen.** Then, as you run out of your favorites, you can test out some of the products I have tried. *I do not use all of the products shown in the list below on a regular basis* or all at once, but out of all the ones I have bought and kept, these are the ones that I feel most comfortable using, knowing that I will get good results. **I admit that I am a product junkie.** However, in a world where a product can be on the shelf one day and discontinued the next, *I like to have choices*, and that is what I am offering you on the next few pages, *choices*. I don't like to be dependent on any one brand/product. So I am hoping the more choices I offer you, the more likely you will be able to find products that work for you in your local beauty supply store. That is one of my main goals – to not have to run all over town looking for products that work.

So with all that said, *in no way am I suggesting that the products I have used/recommend are the only ones that can help you have healthier hair – everyone's hair is different.* However, if you are starting your regimen from scratch or you don't currently like the products you are using, or you just want to try something new, you can choose products from the lists provided as needed. *Buy only what you need to get started* (e.g., maybe 1 shampoo, 1 conditioner, 1 or 2 leave-ins, etc.), and add items as you need to – take it from a woman who has a big bag of products collecting dust in her bathroom (I won't name any names)! *So my warning is to take your time, and buy with care.*

Okay, here is the moment that a lot of ladies are looking forward to – *where I give actual product names!* Well, because I aim to please, I am *sharing* the names of the shampoos, conditioners, leave-in treatments and appliances that I have used or am currently using. I wish I could say that the manufacturers were paying me a lot of money to mention their products, *but they are not!* These are all products that I have tried on my own and liked, and I thought some of you might like them as well. This information is meant to give you products to check out or evaluate as you decide which ones to use in your shampooing and conditioning regimen. Just because I am sharing a lot of information, I can't say this enough: **Please do not buy all of these products!** *You certainly don't need all of them,* probably not even half of them – *you only need a few items from each category.*

Note: The majority of these products can be purchased from local beauty supply stores, salons or online stores. Also, before shopping for any of these products, be sure to check the Daily Hair Care shopping list in Chapter 5 because you may also need a few items for daily maintenance.

Shampoos:

I know there are so many shampoos on the market, but I recommend you **select at least 2** that you can rotate throughout your regimen. To help in your selection, I will list the ones I have used at different points in my regimen in case you decide to try them:

- **Crème of Nature Ultra Moisturizing Formula for Dry, Brittle or Color-Treated Hair Detangling Conditioning Shampoo**
- **KeraCare Hydrating Detangling Shampoo** – usually sold in salons or in online stores such as www.sheldeez.com or www.discount-beauty.com
- **Aubrey Organics Blue Camomile Shampoo** – this is a shampoo that I just started using, but it is all natural, and it has such wonderful ingredients. It can be found in most health food stores or online stores such as www.aubrey-organics.com. Also try 1-800-AUBREY H.
- **Roux Porosity Control Shampoo** – I just started using this occasionally for mid-week shampoos, and I absolutely love it! It's especially for relaxed and color-treated hair and is designed not to strip natural oils.
- **Aveda Sap Moss Shampoo** – Aveda products can be expensive, but some salons sell sample sizes for about $3. Visit www.aveda.com.
- **ION's Anti-Chlorine Swimmer's Shampoo** – only needed if you swim. I have only been able to find this at Sally Beauty Supply.
- **Aubrey Organics Island Naturals Island Butter Shampoo** – I've only been using this shampoo for a short time (mostly after swimming), but I have heard some people rave about it, and it is all natural. The fact that it contains protein may affect the decisions you make regarding leave-in treatments, especially if you suffer from dry or brittle hair. It can be found in most health food stores or online stores such as www.aubrey-organics.com. Also try 1-800-AUBREY H.
- **ApHOGEE Shampoo For Damaged Hair** – I used to use this in Week 4 of my regimen, but now I only plan to use it if I do the Aphogee Treatment for Damaged Hair (an intensive treatment that *claims* to prevent breakage for 6 weeks).

Note: *Although, I have used and recommended Motions At Home Lavish Conditioning Shampoo in the first edition of this book. I have replaced it in my regimen because it contains a **potentially** irritating and drying sudsing agent, sodium lauryl sulfate, as many popular shampoos do. Although I still think it is an okay shampoo (it worked for me in the past), if you suffer from dryness or have scalp sensitivities, like me, you may want to add a little oil to it before using (e.g., jojoba, rosehip, or almond, etc.).*

Conditioners:

I know this is an area where I am a true product junkie, but there are so many good conditioners out there that I could never pick just one! Although I have used all of the following conditioners in my regimen, at different points, *you don't have to* – I just tried them, *liked* them and kept them (most products last a while, and I don't throw anything away unless it is bad)! With that said, I do recommend that you **select at least 2** or **3** conditioners from the following list or of your own choosing:

- **ApHOGEE Intensive Two Minute Keratin Reconstructor**
- **Healthier Hair in a Bottle! Hot Oil Treatment** – can be ordered from www.blackwomansguide.com.
- **Aubrey Organics GPB (Glycogen Protein Balancer) Hair Conditioner and Nutrient** – This product is a new, although pricey, addition to my regimen. It has all natural ingredients, and it is a protein conditioner that does not have an unpleasant smell or make your hair hard/brittle. It can be found in most health food stores or visit www.aubrey-organics.com. Also try 1-800-AUBREY H.
- **Fantasia's Aloe/Vitamin Anti-Breakage Formula Deep Penetrating Crème Moisturizer For Extra Dry Hair & Scalp**
- **Organic Root Stimulator Hair Mayonnaise Treatment for Damaged Hair**
- **Motions Critical Protection & Repair (CPR)**
- **KeraCare Humecto Crème Conditioner** – usually sold in salons or can be ordered from online stores such as www.sheldeez.com or www.discount-beauty.com.
- **Roux Porosity Control pH 4.5 Corrector & Conditioner** – I just started using this occasionally for mid-week shampoos/conditioning, and I absolutely love it! It's especially for relaxed and color-treated hair, and it detangles, moisturizes and makes color more vibrant.
- **Ensure Acidifying Conditioner & Detangler** – mainly meant for ladies whose hair gets very tangled. This product can help to minimize the breakage experienced by some during the after-shampoo comb-out. I have used it mostly after swimming.
- **Aveda Sap Moss Conditioning Detangler** – Visit www.aveda.com or select salons. Some salons also sell samples for $3.
- **ION's Anti-Chlorine Swimmer's Conditioner** – *only needed if you swim*. I have only been able to find this at Sally Beauty Supply.
- **ION's Hard Water Conditioner** – I just recently tried this after swimming, and it helped minimize tangling and breakage during my wet comb-outs.
- **ApHOGEE Balancing Moisturizer** – I used to use this in Week 4 of my regimen, but now I only plan to use it if I do the Aphogee Treatment for Damaged Hair (an intensive treatment that *claims* to prevent breakage for 6 weeks).

Note: *Even though I have recommended and used tcb's Naturals Hot Oil Treatment in the past, I no longer use it in my regimen. I still think it is a decent product, but I noticed that mineral oil is one of the top ingredients, and it also contains 2 different kinds of alcohol. I can't even begin to imagine why that is the case, but I know I don't need that, which is why I developed an all-natural one for myself!*

Leave-In Treatments

I believe there are more leave-in treatments on the market for us than any other item, and I bet I have tried almost all of them! As a result, I can never just stop with one or two. However, you can look at the ones I use, and select **at least 1** or **2** from the following list based on your hair type and method of drying (I have used as many as 4 or 5, but *the number you use is up to you*):

- ***Aphogee Pro-Vitamin Leave-In Conditioner** – works well for all hair types, especially for those who blow or air dry. It also claims to protect color, which is a good thing for those of us hiding gray!
- ***Infusium 23 Leave-In Treatment Original Formula for Damaged Hair** – works well for various hair types, especially relaxed hair.
- ***ApHOGEE Keratin & Green Tea Restructurizer** – great for color and chemically treated hair.
- **John Frieda Frizz-Ease Hair Serum** or **Fantasia Frizz Buster Serum** or **Fantasia Hair Polisher**, *Daily Hair Treatment* – I have used all 3 of these products with great success. I think they all work, which one *you* choose should be based on your personal preference. Having at least one of them is a great "nice-to-have" when you are air drying relaxed hair, especially if your hair/ends are prone to frizz. It works just as well for sisters with naturally curly hair who want to wear straight styles or have problems with frizz.
- **Healthier Hair in a Bottle! Moisturizing & Detangling Mist** – This product helps me get my hair smooth and tangle-free as I am air drying. It can be purchased from www.blackwomansguide.com.
- **Healthier Hair in a Bottle! Oil Spray** – essential if you plan to air dry relaxed hair, it helps seal in moisture and gives it a nice healthy sheen. *In the first edition of this book, I recommended and used Wild Growth Hair Oil for this purpose, but have since stopped using it because of the smell, the mess, and the absence of essential oils.* However, one of these oils will be needed to air dry relaxed hair straight. This product is also great for detangling, softening and adding shine to natural hair. It can be ordered from www.blackwomansguide.com. **Because this product contains Rosemary and Clary Sage, pregnant ladies should check with their ob/gyn before using, or use Wild Growth instead.**
- **Lottabody's Straight Stuff Temporary Straightening Conditioner** – helpful if you plan to air dry or blow dry your hair. This product used to be sold at Sally's, but now I can only find it at the occasional beauty supply store or www.ebonyline.com/hair-care-by-brand-lottabody.html. If you can't find it, an alternate product is tcb's Bone Strait Conditioner & Blow Dry Lotion.
- **Nu Expressions Moisturizing Foam Wrapping Lotion** – I have to say that this has become my favorite leave-in treatment. It works wonders in terms of detangling and air drying. It's hard to find though, try salons or call 1-888-Salon99.
- **Salon Finish For Silky Hair Foam Wrap & Style Lotion** – I had been using this product for detangling, and it replaced a lot of the other leave-in treatments I used to use. It works great for air drying as well as for wet sets and blow drying. I only plan to use it now if I run out of the Nu Expressions product.
- **Roux Fanci-Full Temporary Hair Color Rinse** – although this is a rinse, it can be used more as a leave-in treatment that temporarily colors the hair or covers/highlights gray (depends on the formula) without damaging effects. It also contains styling lotion. So far I love it! No more semi-permanent color for me!
- **911 Emergency Leave-In Conditioner** – I used this product when I first developed my regimen, and I liked it, but I just stopped using it as I tried other products. I have heard good reports on it from women with natural hair.

NOTE: *The products marked with an asterisk contain various forms of protein, which is something you should keep in mind as you decide which one(s) to use on various weeks. As an example if for Week 1 or Week 3 you use a conditioner containing protein (e.g., reconstructor or GPB), you may not want to use leave-in treatments containing protein. I mention it because some people's hair can get hard/brittle if too many products containing protein are used at once – it took me a while to notice that mine does. So if you notice a problem, you can make adjustments as needed.*

Appliances & Related Products

These items are optional based on your plans for deep conditioning and setting your hair. Only buy these additional items if you *really* need them.

- **Heating Cap** or **Hooded Dryer** – Necessary for deep conditioning, but some people get away with using a hot towel (very inconvenient and not as effective) or a shower cap while showering. It is entirely up to you. The dryer can also obviously be used for wet sets. I have used both with success, so the choice is yours. However, if you choose the heating cap, *be sure to read the manufacturer's instructions before using.*
- **Plastic Cap** (not a traditional shower cap/bonnet, but a thin see-through plastic cap, with loose elastic, often called processing caps) – Necessary if you plan to deep condition your hair by sitting under a heating cap or dryer. Buy a pack of them (the complimentary ones found in hotels are better because they are very loose fitting) for deep conditioning, overnight use and for use under tight fitting wigs or hats to seal in moisture.
- **Ionic Blow Dryer** (Conair, Ion, Revlon and Vidal Sassoon make them) – If you cannot be talked out of blow drying your hair on a regular basis, try a *potentially* safer alternative. I have never tried it, so *use with care...*
- **Caruso Steam Hair Setter** – A nice-to-have if you plan to set/curl your hair after air or blow drying (replaces curling irons and electric curlers).

I know this list may be overwhelming at first, but I am only *sharing* the names of products that I have personally used with good results or have heard other women give good reports on. *You do not have to buy all of these products to have a successful regimen. In fact, you don't have to use **any** of them if you already have a list of favorites that work for you, which is what good hair care is about anyway – finding out what works for Y-O-U and doing it consistently.* So with that said, as you go to your local beauty supply store, read the labels for any of the products I mentioned that sound interesting to you. I am only suggesting that you **purchase the minimum number of products needed for your hair type and routine.** My goal is to assist you in customizing your own personalized regimen, using my week-by-week framework as an example to help you make your product selections. I say buy the minimum number of products because **you can always add other products later, as necessary.**

I am not trying to get anyone to become a product junkie like me – I am just sharing information so you can avoid wasting money on products like I have done in the past. So with this in mind, accept my recommendations in this section as a warm referral on products that you *may* need/want for your regimen. However, if you do wind up buying some of the products I mentioned, keep in mind that most of them last from three to six months, or longer (especially the appliances). So you can think of any purchases you make as an initial investment that will give you all the tools you need to sustain the *Six-Week Regimen* for months, with only a few replacement purchases during the year.

Finally, to assist you, I will repeat the shampooing and conditioning directions each week in the regimen, with the appropriate product substitutions. However, you will have to go to Chapter 4 for drying methods (e.g., air drying, wet sets, etc...). As you follow the regimen, please keep in mind that *results may vary if products/substitutions are made or if steps are skipped. While you do have the option to change the regimen however you wish, realize that your tweaks could produce different results.* With all that said, let's get started with Week1!

WEEK 1

Restore!

The steps shown below describe my first at-home shampoo after a touch-up, usually done one week after. This week's goal is to restore our hair – its moisture, life and vitality! If your hair is relaxed, this is a great restorative treatment for the week after it has been chemically-treated. However, if your hair is natural, this is a wonderful way to restore strength, softness and elasticity to dry, brittle hair. Regardless of your hair type, this treatment can help improve the condition and appearance of hair that has been damaged or abused. I like to think of it as a rebuilding step for our hair, whether it is healthy or damaged, which is a great way to kick off a brand new hair care regimen, *which is what I hope you are doing*!

Shampooing & Conditioning Steps

1. **Rinse** hair thoroughly with warm water, and **shampoo** with **KeraCare Hydrating Detangling Shampoo** or the shampoo of your choice according to the directions on the back of the bottle. *If a sufficient lather is created (it should be if you thoroughly wet your hair first), and your hair is not excessively dirty or sticky from product build-up, only lather once.* Rinse hair thoroughly and gently towel dry.

2. **Apply** a generous amount of **ApHOGEE Intensive Two Minute Keratin Reconstructor** or the conditioner of your choice. Work it evenly through the hair, from roots to ends, concentrating on the ends and **avoiding the scalp**. DO NOT RINSE. **Note:** *If your hair is in pretty good condition, you may not need this extra conditioning step. If so, proceed to step 3, below. However, if your hair is like mine, and it needs all the help it can get, this extra step works wonders.*

3. Next, **apply** a small amount of **KeraCare Humecto Crème Conditioner** or the crème conditioner of your choice, and work it evenly through hair, concentrating on the ends and avoiding the scalp. Afterwards, twist or smooth the hair to the top of your head, making sure that the ends and edges are well covered with conditioner. Again, do not rinse.

4. **Cover hair** with a plastic cap, and sit either under a dryer or a heating cap for at least 15 to 30 minutes, depending on the condition and texture of your hair. The conditioners I have recommended are heat-activated. Therefore, the longer heat is applied, the more conditioning your hair receives. For those with fine hair or hair that is not damaged or subjected to constant heat styling and abuse, 15 minutes or less may be sufficient. However, if more conditioning is needed, increase the time spent under the heating cap or dryer accordingly. Because my hair is coarse and prone to dryness, I try to stay under for at least 30 minutes, and the benefits are phenomenal! For people with dryness, breakage or damaged hair, this step is critical, and the longer heat is applied, the better. *However, I do not recommend more than 45 minutes.* **WARNING:** *Please be sure to follow ALL of the manufacturer's instructions for your heating cap or dryer.* There may be special warnings for people with certain illnesses or conditions (e.g., diabetes or circulatory problems).

5. **Rinse** hair thoroughly, first with warm water and finally with cool water. Then, gently towel hair dry.

6. **Apply** your favorite leave-in treatment(s) to your hair. I use **Healthier Hair in a Bottle! Moisturizing & Detangling Mist** and **Nu Expressions Moisturizing Foam Wrapping** Lotion by Bronner Brothers. I also just started using **Roux Fanci-Full Temporary Hair Color Rinse** (Formula 12 Black Rage) to cover my gray. For each of the products applied, let the length of your hair determine the amount you use. DO NOT SATURATE HAIR WITH ANY OF THE PRODUCTS, and do not rinse.

    IMPORTANT NOTE: If you plan to dry your hair by wrapping, roller, spiral or straw setting, you may want to substitute the setting lotion of your choice (e.g., Lottabody Texturizing Setting Lotion, Nu Expressions Moisturizing Foam Wrapping Lotion, Salon Finish For Silky Hair Foam Wrap & Style Lotion, etc.) for one or more of your leave-in treatments.

7. Gently **comb** through hair with a wide-tooth comb. Start at the ends and gently detangle, working from the ends to the root. Never comb hair from the roots to the ends without detangling first. Your hair is very fragile when it is wet, so handle it with care. Also, do not brush hair to remove tangles. Part the hair into four to six sections, and clip each section after combing, if necessary.

8. Go to Chapter 4 for tips on various drying methods (e.g., air drying, wet sets, etc.).

NOTES FROM WEEK 1

Substitutions:

Shampoo: _____

Conditioners: _____

_____

Leave-In Treatments: _____

_____

_____

_____

Additional Comments:

_____

_____

_____

_____

WEEK 2

Revitalize!

Given the fact that our hair is exposed to sun, wind and pollution on a daily basis, not to mention to heat appliances such as curling irons, is it any wonder that it can get a little dry and dull? As a result, every so often, our hair may need a little pick-me-up. Well, get ready for a treat because this week's goal is to revitalize our hair, giving it a soft, healthy look and *feel*, as well as improving overall manageability. After completing the steps for this week my hair is *bouncy*, *full* and *soft*, I think yours will be too!

Shampooing & Conditioning Steps

Note: Step 2 (below) can be done before or after shampooing. Although I do it in the order shown below, there are some women who may not suffer from dryness, and they may benefit more from doing the hot oil treatment before the shampoo. Because every woman is different, I say let your hair be your guide. However, here is what I do...

1. **Rinse** hair thoroughly with warm water, and **shampoo** with **Crème of Nature Ultra Moisturizing Formula for Dry, Brittle or Color-Treated Hair Detangling Conditioning Shampoo** or the shampoo of your choice according to the directions on the back of the bottle. *If a sufficient lather is created (it should be if you thoroughly wet your hair first), and your hair is not excessively dirty or sticky from product build-up, only lather once.* Rinse hair and gently towel dry.

2. **Place** a bottle of **Healthier Hair in a Bottle! Hot Oil Treatment** or the hot oil product of your choice (e.g., tcb Naturals Hot Oil Treatment, etc.) in a glass of hot water. When the bottle/tube feels hot, put a small amount of oil in your hands, and work it evenly through hair and into the scalp. Make sure ends are well covered. I only use about ¼ to ½ ounce. Unless your hair is extremely long and/or thick, I recommend you use only as much as you need to cover your hair. For shorter lengths, you can use even less if your hair seems sufficiently covered. The amount you use is up to you. DO NOT RINSE.

3. Next, if extra conditioning is desired, **apply** a small amount of the crème conditioner of your choice (I used to use Motions, but now I use **KeraCare Humecto Crème Conditioner**). Work it evenly through the hair, from roots to ends, concentrating on the ends, but *avoiding the scalp*. Again, do not rinse. **Note:** *If your hair is in pretty good condition, you may not need this extra conditioning step. However, if your hair is like mine, and it needs all the help it can get, this step works wonders.*

4. **Cover hair** with a plastic cap, and sit either under a dryer or a heating cap for at least 15 to 30 minutes, depending on the condition and texture of your hair. The conditioners I have recommended are heat-activated. Therefore, the longer heat is applied, the more conditioning your hair receives. For those with fine hair or hair that is not damaged or subjected to constant heat styling and abuse, 15 minutes or less may be sufficient. However, if more conditioning is needed, increase the time spent under the heating cap or dryer accordingly. Because my hair is coarse and prone to dryness, I try to stay under my dryer for at least 30 minutes, and the benefits are phenomenal! For people with dryness, breakage or damaged hair, this step is critical, and the longer heat is applied, the better. *However, I do not recommend more than 45 minutes.* **WARNING: *Please be sure to follow ALL of the manufacturer's instructions for your heating cap or***

dryer. There may be special warnings for people with certain illnesses or conditions (e.g., diabetes or circulatory problems).

5. **Rinse** hair thoroughly, first with warm water (as warm as you can stand to remove excess oil) and finally with cool water. An extra rinse or two may be necessary, as you want to remove the oil. Then, gently towel hair dry.

6. **Apply** your favorite leave-in treatment(s) to your hair. I use **Healthier Hair in a Bottle! Moisturizing & Detangling Mist** and **Nu Expressions Moisturizing Foam Wrapping Lotion** by Bronner Brothers. I also just started using **Roux Fanci-Full Temporary Hair Color Rinse** (Formula 12 Black Rage) to cover my gray. For each of the products applied, let the length of your hair determine the amount you use. DO NOT SATURATE HAIR WITH ANY OF THE PRODUCTS, and do not rinse.

   IMPORTANT NOTE: If you plan to dry your hair by wrapping, roller, spiral or straw setting, you may want to substitute the setting lotion of your choice (e.g., Lottabody Texturizing Setting Lotion, Nu Expressions Moisturizing Foam Wrapping Lotion, Salon Finish For Silky Hair Foam Wrap & Style Lotion, etc.) for one or more of your leave-in treatments.

7. Gently **comb** through hair with a wide-tooth comb. Start at the ends and gently detangle, working from the ends to the root. Never comb hair from the roots to the ends without detangling first. Your hair is very fragile when it is wet, so handle it with care. Also, do not brush hair to remove tangles. Part the hair into four to six sections, and clip each section after combing, if necessary.

8. Go to Chapter 4 for tips on various drying methods (e.g., air drying, wet sets, etc.).

NOTES FROM WEEK 2

Substitutions:

Shampoo: _____

Conditioners: _____

_____

Leave-In Treatments: _____

_____

_____

_____

Additional Comments:

_____

_____

_____

_____

WEEK 3

Replenish!

Hopefully you had a great hair week! However, just in case things didn't go as well as you would have liked with your daily regimen, this week's goal is to make up for it, strengthening your hair, while replenishing its natural moisture and shine. Even if you had a great hair week, our hair can always use a boost. As a result of this week's treatment your hair should *look* and *feel* thicker, and it should have plenty of body *and* sheen.

Shampooing & Conditioning Steps

1. **Rinse** hair thoroughly with warm water, and **shampoo** with **Aubrey Organics Blue Camomile Shampoo** or the shampoo of your choice according to the directions on the back of the bottle. *If a sufficient lather is created (it should be if you thoroughly wet your hair first), and your hair is not excessively dirty or sticky from product build-up, **only lather once**.* Rinse hair and gently towel dry.

2. **Apply Aubrey Organics GPB (Glycogen Protein Balancer) Hair Conditioner and Nutrient** to your hands. Work it evenly through the hair, avoiding the scalp and concentrating on the ends. DO NOT RINSE.

3. Next, if extra conditioning and moisturizing is needed, you may also apply a small amount of **KeraCare Humecto Crème Conditioner** or the crème conditioner of your choice to the hair and ends. I do this now because although protein strengthens, it can be drying for some. This extra step gives the best of both worlds – *strength plus moisture*. Again, do not rinse. **Note:** This step can also be done **after** rinsing the GPB conditioner out.

4. **Cover hair** with a plastic cap, and sit either under a dryer or a heating cap for at least 15 to 30 minutes, depending on the condition and texture of your hair. For those with fine hair or hair that is **not** damaged or subjected to constant heat styling and abuse, you can shorten the time spent under the dryer/heating cap to 10 to 15 minutes, or it can be left on the hair **without** heat for 10 minutes. **WARNING:** *Please be sure to follow ALL of the manufacturer's instructions for your heating cap or dryer.* There may be special warnings for people with certain illnesses or conditions (e.g., diabetes or circulatory problems).

5. **Rinse** hair thoroughly, first with warm water and finally with cool water. Then, gently towel hair dry.

6. **Apply** your favorite leave-in treatment(s) to your hair. I use **Healthier Hair in a Bottle! Moisturizing & Detangling Mist** and **Nu Expressions Moisturizing Foam Wrapping Lotion** by Bronner Brothers. I also just started using **Roux Fanci-Full Temporary Hair Color Rinse** (Formula 12 Black Rage) to cover my gray. For each of the products applied, let the length of your hair determine the amount you use. DO NOT SATURATE HAIR WITH ANY OF THE PRODUCTS, and do not rinse.

   IMPORTANT NOTE: If you plan to dry your hair by wrapping, roller, spiral or straw setting, you may want to substitute the setting lotion of your choice (e.g., Lottabody Texturizing Setting Lotion, Nu Expressions Moisturizing Foam Wrapping Lotion, Salon Finish For Silky Hair Foam Wrap & Style Lotion, etc.) for one or more of your leave-in treatments.

7. Gently **comb** through hair with a wide-tooth comb. Start at the ends and gently detangle, working from the ends to the root. Never comb hair from the roots to the ends without detangling first. Your hair is very fragile when it is wet, so handle it with care. Also, do not brush hair to remove tangles. Part the hair into four to six sections, and clip each section after combing, if necessary.

8. Go to Chapter 4 for tips on various drying methods (e.g., air drying, wet sets, etc.).

NOTES FROM WEEK 3

Substitutions:

Shampoo: _____

Conditioners: _____

_____

Leave-In Treatments: _____

_____

_____

_____

Additional Comments:

_____

_____

_____

_____

WEEK 4

Repair!

No matter how careful we are, there are times when we subject our hair to some sort of abuse (e.g., heat styling, rough combing, use of alcohol-based hair sprays and gels, etc.), *even if we don't realize it.* With these times in mind, this week's goal is to repair and protect our hair, helping return it to a healthier, stronger condition and to its natural beauty. As a result, our hair should be moisturized, strengthened and more manageable after this week's treatment.

Shampooing & Conditioning Steps

1. **Rinse** hair thoroughly with warm water, and **shampoo** with **Crème of Nature Ultra Moisturizing Formula for Dry, Brittle or Color-Treated Hair Detangling Conditioning Shampoo** or the shampoo of your choice according to the directions on the back of the bottle. *If a sufficient lather is created (it should be if you thoroughly wet your hair first), and your hair is not excessively dirty or sticky from product build-up, only lather once.* Rinse hair and gently towel dry.

2. **Apply Fantasia's Aloe/Vitamin Anti-Breakage Formula Deep Penetrating Crème Moisturizer For Extra Dry Hair & Scalp**. Work it evenly through the hair, from roots to ends, **avoiding the scalp** and concentrating on the ends. DO NOT RINSE.

3. **Cover hair** with a plastic cap, and sit either under a dryer or a heating cap for at least 15 to 30 minutes, depending on the condition and texture of your hair. The conditioners I have recommended are heat-activated. Therefore, the longer heat is applied, the more conditioning your hair receives. For those with fine hair or hair that is not damaged or subjected to constant heat styling and abuse, 15 minutes or less may be sufficient. However, if more conditioning is needed, increase the time spent under the heating cap or dryer accordingly. Because my hair is coarse and prone to dryness, I try to stay under my dryer for at least 30 minutes, and the benefits are phenomenal! For people with dryness, breakage or damaged hair, this step is critical, and the longer heat is applied, the better. *However, I do not recommend more than 45 minutes.* **WARNING: *Please be sure to follow ALL of the manufacturer's instructions for your heating cap or dryer.*** There may be special warnings for people with certain illnesses or conditions (e.g., diabetes or circulatory problems).

4. **Rinse** hair thoroughly, first with warm water and finally with cool water. Then, gently towel hair dry.

5. **Apply** your favorite leave-in treatment(s) to your hair. I use **Healthier Hair in a Bottle! Moisturizing & Detangling Mist** and **Nu Expressions Moisturizing Foam Wrapping Lotion** by Bronner Brothers. I also just started using **Roux Fanci-Full Temporary Hair Color Rinse** (Formula 12 Black Rage) to cover my gray. For each of the products applied, let the length of your hair determine the amount you use. DO NOT SATURATE HAIR WITH ANY OF THE PRODUCTS, and do not rinse.

   IMPORTANT NOTE: If you plan to dry your hair by wrapping, roller, spiral or straw setting, you may want to substitute the setting lotion of your choice (e.g., Lottabody Texturizing Setting Lotion, Nu Expressions Moisturizing Foam Wrapping Lotion, Salon Finish For Silky Hair Foam Wrap & Style Lotion, etc.) for one or more of your leave-in treatments.

6. Gently **comb** through hair with a wide-tooth comb. Start at the ends and gently detangle, working from the ends to the root. Never comb hair from the roots to the ends without detangling first. Your hair is very fragile when it is wet, so handle it with care. Also, do not brush hair to remove tangles. Part the hair into four to six sections, and clip each section after combing, if necessary.

7. Go to Chapter 4 for tips on various drying methods (e.g., air drying, wet sets, etc.).

NOTES FROM WEEK 4

Substitutions:

Shampoo: _____

Conditioners: _____

_____

Leave-In Treatments: _____

_____

_____

_____

Additional Comments:

_____

_____

_____

_____

WEEK 5

Rejuvenate!

This week's goal is to rejuvenate dull, lifeless hair that has been subjected to a month's worth of environmental exposure, combing, brushing and heat styling. As a result of this week's treatment, dry, brittle hair will get a boost while you receive protection from heat damage and split-ends. After this week's treatment, my hair feels *so good* that I sometimes forget that I am five weeks into my relaxer! Regardless of your hair type, your hair should be easier to style, and it should be more vibrant, bouncy and healthy-looking.

Shampooing & Conditioning Steps

1. **Rinse** hair thoroughly with warm water, and **shampoo** with **KeraCare Hydrating Detangling Shampoo** or the shampoo of your choice according to the directions on the back of the bottle. *If a sufficient lather is created (it should be if you thoroughly wet your hair first), and your hair is not excessively dirty or sticky from product build-up, **only lather once**.* Rinse hair and gently towel dry.

2. **Apply Organic Root Stimulator Hair Mayonnaise Treatment for Damaged Hair**. Work it evenly through the hair, from roots to ends, **avoiding the scalp** and concentrating on the ends. DO NOT RINSE.

3. If extra conditioning and moisturizing is desired, **apply** a small amount of **KeraCare Humecto Crème Conditioner** or the crème conditioner of your choice. Work it evenly through the hair, from roots to ends, avoiding the scalp and concentrating on the ends. Again, do not rinse.

4. **Cover hair** with a plastic cap, and sit either under a dryer or a heating cap for at least 15 to 30 minutes, depending on the condition and texture of your hair. The conditioners I have recommended are heat-activated. Therefore, the longer heat is applied, the more conditioning your hair receives. For those with fine hair or hair that is not damaged or subjected to constant heat styling and abuse, 15 minutes or less may be sufficient. However, if more conditioning is needed, increase the time spent under the heating cap or dryer accordingly. Because my hair is coarse and prone to dryness, I try to stay under my dryer for at least 30 minutes. For people with dryness, breakage or damaged hair, this step is critical, and the longer heat is applied, the better. *However, I do not recommend more than 45 minutes.* **WARNING:** *Please be sure to follow ALL of the manufacturer's instructions for your heating cap or dryer.* There may be special warnings for people with certain illnesses or conditions (e.g., diabetes or circulatory problems).

5. **Rinse** hair thoroughly, first with warm water and finally with cool water. Then, gently towel hair dry.

6. **Apply** your favorite leave-in treatment(s) to your hair. I use **Healthier Hair in a Bottle! Moisturizing & Detangling Mist** and **Nu Expressions Moisturizing Foam Wrapping Lotion** by Bronner Brothers. I also just started using **Roux Fanci-Full Temporary Hair Color Rinse (Formula 12 Black Rage)** to cover my gray. For each of the products applied, let the length of your hair determine the amount you use. DO NOT SATURATE HAIR WITH ANY OF THE PRODUCTS, and do not rinse.

    IMPORTANT NOTE: If you plan to dry your hair by wrapping, roller, spiral or straw setting, you may want to substitute the setting lotion of your choice (e.g., Lottabody Texturizing Setting Lotion, Nu Expressions

Moisturizing Foam Wrapping Lotion, Salon Finish For Silky Hair Foam Wrap & Style Lotion, etc.) for one or more of your leave-in treatments.

7.   Gently **comb** through hair with a wide-tooth comb. Start at the ends and gently detangle, working from the ends to the root. Never comb hair from the roots to the ends without detangling first. Your hair is very fragile when it is wet, so handle it with care. Also, do not brush hair to remove tangles. Part the hair into four to six sections, and clip each section after combing, if necessary.

8.   Go to Chapter 4 for tips on various drying methods (e.g., air drying, wet sets, etc.).

NOTES FROM WEEK 5

<u>Substitutions:</u>

Shampoo: _____

Conditioners: _____

_____

Leave-In Treatments: _____

_____

_____

_____

<u>Additional Comments:</u>

_____

_____

_____

_____

WEEK 6

Resuscitate!

For many women, this is the week before a touch-up. *Hopefully no one has broken down and had one sooner – I have made that **MISTAKE** too many times myself.* I had gotten to the point where I rarely made it to Week 6 in my first book. However, some noticeable thinning and breakage was enough to give me a major wake-up call, and now, not only do I *make it* to this week, I go at least 12 weeks (sometimes longer) before relaxing. Well, regardless of how long you wait or whether your hair is relaxed or natural, I bet your hair could use a little resuscitation or a breath of life right about now. If so, I have great news for you! This week's goal is to revive, protect and improve the overall health of your hair, regardless of its type. My hair is so soft and shiny afterwards that I almost forget that I am 6 weeks into my relaxer! This treatment also helps to minimize breakage, which is really great news for ladies who will be relaxing soon.

Shampooing & Conditioning Steps

1. **Rinse** hair thoroughly with warm water, and **shampoo** with **Crème of Nature Ultra Moisturizing Formula for Dry, Brittle or Color-Treated Hair Detangling Conditioning Shampoo** or the shampoo of your choice according to the directions on the back of the bottle. *If a sufficient lather is created (it should be if you thoroughly wet your hair first), and your hair is not excessively dirty or sticky from product build-up, **only lather once**.* Rinse hair and gently towel dry.

2. **Apply Motions Critical Protection & Repair (CPR)**. Work it evenly through the hair, from roots to ends, **avoiding the scalp** and concentrating on the ends. DO NOT RINSE.

3. For extra conditioning, you may also apply a small amount of **KeraCare Humecto Crème Conditioner** or the crème conditioner of your choice to the hair and ends. I always do this, and the results are fantastic. Again, do not rinse.

4. **Cover hair** with a plastic cap, and sit either under a dryer or a heating cap for at least 15 to 30 minutes, depending on the condition and texture of your hair. The conditioners I have recommended are heat-activated. Therefore, the longer heat is applied, the more conditioning your hair receives. For those with fine hair or hair that is not damaged or subjected to constant heat styling and abuse, 15 minutes or less may be sufficient. However, if more conditioning is needed, increase the time spent under the heating cap or dryer accordingly. Because my hair is coarse and prone to dryness, I try to stay under my dryer for at least 30 minutes. For people with dryness, breakage or damaged hair, this step is critical, and the longer heat is applied, the better. *However, I do not recommend more than 45 minutes.* **WARNING: *Please be sure to follow ALL of the manufacturer's instructions for your heating cap or dryer.*** There may be special warnings for people with certain illnesses or conditions (e.g., diabetes or circulatory problems).

5. **Rinse** hair thoroughly, first with warm water and finally with cool water. Then, gently towel hair dry.

6. **Apply** your favorite leave-in treatment(s) to your hair. I use **Healthier Hair in a Bottle! Moisturizing & Detangling Mist** and **Nu Expressions Moisturizing Foam Wrapping Lotion** by Bronner Brothers. I also just started using **Roux Fanci-Full Temporary Hair Color Rinse** (Formula 12 Black Rage) to cover my gray. For each of the products applied, let the length of your hair determine the amount you use. DO NOT SATURATE HAIR WITH ANY OF THE PRODUCTS, and do not rinse.

   IMPORTANT NOTE: If you plan to dry your hair by wrapping, roller, spiral or straw setting, you may want to substitute the setting lotion of your choice (e.g., Lottabody Texturizing Setting Lotion, Nu Expressions Moisturizing Foam Wrapping Lotion, Salon Finish For Silky Hair Foam Wrap & Style Lotion, etc.) for one or more of your leave-in treatments.

7. Gently **comb** through hair with a wide-tooth comb. Start at the ends and gently detangle, working from the ends to the root. Never comb hair from the roots to the ends without detangling first. Your hair is very fragile when it is wet, so handle it with care. Also, do not brush hair to remove tangles. Part the hair into four to six sections, and clip each section after combing, if necessary.

8. Go to Chapter 4 for tips on various drying methods (e.g., air drying, wet sets, etc.).

NOTES FROM WEEK 6

Substitutions:

Shampoo: _____

Conditioners: _____

_____

Leave-In Treatments: _____

_____

_____

_____

Additional Comments:

_____

_____

_____

_____

SIX-WEEK REGIMEN
REMINDERS

SHAMPOO & DEEP CONDITION WITH:

Week 1:   KeraCare Hydrating Detangling Shampoo
ApHOGEE Intensive Two Minute Keratin Reconstructor **&**
KeraCare Humecto Crème Conditioner (optional)

OR

_____

_____

_____

Week 2:   Crème of Nature Ultra Moisturizing Formula for Dry, Brittle or Color-Treated Hair Detangling
Conditioning Shampoo
Healthier Hair in a Bottle! Hot Oil Treatment **&**
KeraCare Humecto Crème Conditioner (optional)
OR

_____

_____

_____

Week 3:   Aubrey Organics Blue Camomile Shampoo **&**
Aubrey Organics GPB (Glycogen Protein Balancer) Hair Conditioner and Nutrient
KeraCare Humecto Crème Conditioner (optional)

OR

_____

_____

_____

Week 4:   Crème of Nature Ultra Moisturizing Formula for Dry, Brittle or Color-Treated Hair Detangling
Conditioning Shampoo **&**
Fantasia's Aloe/Vitamin Anti-Breakage Formula Deep Penetrating Crème Moisturizer For Extra
Dry Hair & Scalp

OR

_____

_____

_____

Week 5:   KeraCare Hydrating Detangling Shampoo
Organic Root Stimulator Hair Mayonnaise Treatment for Damaged Hair **&**
KeraCare Humecto Crème Conditioner (optional)

OR

_____

_____

_____

Week 6:   Crème of Nature Ultra Moisturizing Formula for Dry, Brittle or Color-Treated Hair Detangling
Conditioning Shampoo
Motions Critical Protection & Repair **&**
KeraCare Humecto Crème Conditioner (optional)

OR

_____

_____

_____

LEAVE-IN TREATMENT/CONDITIONERS:

After rinsing, apply **your** favorite leave-in(s). Make your selection based on your hair's type, condition and drying method. I use the following products in my personal regimen:

- Healthier Hair in a Bottle! Moisturizing & Detangling Mist
- Nu Expressions Moisturizing Foam Wrapping Lotion
- Roux Fanci-Full Temporary Hair Color Rinse

OR

- _____
- _____
- _____

REPEAT

After completing the steps outlined in Week 6, I **used** to run to my hair stylist for a touch-up, *sometimes even a week before*. However, I have since turned from my wicked ways (I am a *recovering* relaxer addict, taking it one week at a time) – it is amazing how fast a little thinning and breakage can wake you up! Now by the time I have a touch-up, I have usually repeated the steps in Weeks 1-6, or *some variation of them*, twice. So if you have relaxed hair you can start back at Week 1 and continue the weeks of the regimen until it is time for your touch-up. Regardless of which week you get a touch-up, remember to pick up wherever you left off in the regimen or just start back at Week 1 again (*this is what I do*). However, ladies with natural hair can continue repeating the six-week cycle (the steps in Weeks 1-6) indefinitely, modifying or switching products as desired.

Did you notice that I said I do *some variation* of the six-week regimen during this repeat phase? Well, sometimes, instead of just repeating the six-week regimen word-for-word, after Week 6, I rotate my favorite shampoos and use other conditioners that I liked, but did not include in the core six weeks of the regimen. I also use this time to *experiment* with new shampoos and conditioners that catch my eye just to make sure I am not missing out on anything. I tried Proclaim's Professional Care Cholesterol at one point for Week 8 (I used to recommend a cholesterol treatment by Dark & Lovely, but I can no longer find it – my overall opinion of the Proclaim product was that it was just *okay*). I also thought of trying the new Pantene line for relaxed and natural hair (*I believe they offer free samples*) as I heard good feedback on a few of the products, but I am not sure after reading some of the ingredients on the back label... However, there are two products that I really want to try: KeraCare's First Lather Shampoo and their Dry & Itchy Scalp Conditioner – so many products, so little time! Another product I am thinking about including at some point after Week 6 is Aphogee's Treatment for Damaged Hair (a very stinky product that makes your hair hard). Although I was less than impressed the first few times I used it, I keep hearing people claim that it really helps to prevent breakage, and a few have even claimed that it can lengthen the time between touch-ups, and I can't wait to see if this is true!

So as you can see, the Repeat phase is a good time to let your product junky side run wild before you go back to the more structured Six-Week Regimen. The good thing about it is if you find a shampoo, conditioner or treatment you like more you can update your core regimen accordingly. As you repeat the *Six-Week Regimen*, month after month, be sure to monitor your hair's overall condition so you can tailor your regimen to meet your hair's changing needs. Make sure that your hair not only looks healthy, but also that it is *improving over time* – you should be experiencing more growth, your ends should be in better shape, and there should not be as much dryness or breakage. However, if you *do not* notice significant improvement over time, you will need to identify what area of your regimen needs *tweaking*. Sometimes, it can be as simple as switching a product or two, a change in drying or styling methods or a change in the types of chemicals applied to your hair (e.g., strong relaxer vs. gentle, or permanent color vs. semi-permanent, etc.). However, if it is not obvious to you, a consultation with a *trusted* hair stylist, dermatologist or internist might be necessary. Depending on the problem you encounter, one of these specialists can hopefully give recommendations for your hair's special or changing needs. I bring the doctors into this because some of the biggest hair problems I have had over the past few years (e.g., thinning/breakage caused by overprocessing and dryness, made worse by chronic, untreated anemia) were pointed out by my dermatologist and internist. Sometimes doctors can look at your personal medical history or symptoms (e.g., stress, anemia, etc.) and recommend changes or medications to help your situation. *Problems caught early are more easily corrected*, so keep your eyes open, and whatever the problem(s), be quick to address and resolve them.

In addition, and more importantly, *if your hair or skin is not responding well to one or more of the products in the regimen as you follow the manufacturer directions, stop using the product(s) immediately*. Also, if you ever have any questions or concerns regarding a reaction to a product, contact a dermatologist or your personal physician immediately.

MID-WEEK/REFRESHER SHAMPOO

Although many of us are satisfied with the once-a-week shampooing/conditioning provided by Weeks 1-6, some of us may find that this is not enough to keep our hair soft and hydrated, especially if it is prone to dryness, oiliness or if we work out on a regular basis. Shortly after I turned 35, I noticed that by the fourth day after a shampoo my hair started to look and feel *bone dry*. Some of this can be attributed to my chronic battle with anemia and temporary laziness about moisturizing, but I think most of it was caused by the fact that my hair now needs to be *hydrated* every 3-4 days. Everyone's hair may not, but for those of you who do, here is a mini-regimen that I follow for my mid-week shampoo:

Shampooing & Conditioning Steps

1. **Rinse** hair thoroughly with warm water, and **shampoo** with a very small amount (I try to use about one capful) of either: **Crème of Nature Ultra Moisturizing Formula for Dry, Brittle or Color-Treated Hair Detangling Conditioning Shampoo; KeraCare Hydrating Detangling Shampoo; Roux Porosity Control Shampoo; Aveda Sap Moss Shampoo**; or **Aubrey Organics Blue Camomile Shampoo** (I alternate shampoos, trying not to use the same one back to back during the week) *or the shampoo of your choice* according to the directions on the back of the bottle. Rinse hair and gently towel dry.

2. **Apply** any one of the crème conditioners you use during your normal six-week regimen. Depending on the shampoo I use, I choose **one** of the following: **Fantasia Aloe/Vitamin Anti-Breakage Formula Deep Penetrating Crème Moisturizer For Extra Dry Hair & Scalp; Motions Critical Protection & Repair; Organic Root Stimulator Hair Mayonnaise Treatment for Damaged Hair; KeraCare Humecto Crème Conditioner; Roux Porosity Control pH 4.5 Corrector & Conditioner; Aveda Sap Moss Conditioning Detangler**; or **Ensure Acidifying Conditioner & Detangler**. Work the conditioner evenly through the hair, from roots to ends, avoiding the scalp and concentrating on the ends. Leave on for a few minutes before rinsing. Because I tend to shampoo in the shower, I usually leave the conditioner on while I get cleaned up (you can put on a shower cap or just pull it up high on your head). Then as I am rinsing off, I rinse the conditioner off too.

3. **Rinse** hair thoroughly, first with warm water and finally with cool water. Then, gently towel hair dry.

4. **Apply** your favorite leave-in treatment(s) to your hair. I use **Healthier Hair in a Bottle! Moisturizing & Detangling Mist** and **Nu Expressions Moisturizing Foam Wrapping Lotion** by Bronner Brothers. I also just started using **Roux Fanci-Full Temporary Hair Color Rinse** (Formula 12 Black Rage) to cover my gray. For each of the products applied, let the length of your hair determine the amount you use. There is no need to saturate your hair with any of these products. Distribute them evenly, and **do not rinse**.

   IMPORTANT NOTE: If you plan to dry your hair by wrapping, roller, spiral or straw setting, you may want to substitute the setting lotion of your choice (e.g., Lottabody Texturizing Setting Lotion, Nu Expressions Moisturizing Foam Wrapping Lotion, Salon Finish For Silky Hair Foam Wrap & Style Lotion, etc.) for one or more of your leave-in treatments.

5. Gently **comb** through hair with a wide-tooth comb. Start at the ends and gently detangle, working from the ends to the root. Never comb hair from the roots to the ends without detangling first. Your hair is very fragile when it is wet, so handle it with care. Also, do not brush hair to remove tangles. Part the hair into four to six sections, and clip each section after combing, if necessary.

6. Go to Chapter 4 for tips on various drying methods (e.g., air drying, wet sets, etc.).

WORK-OUT/MID-WEEK
CONDITIONING RINSE

So many ladies have written me over the years asking for tips on how to maintain their hair when they work out. Just like with swimming, many of us have avoided regular exercise routines because of the hassle of keeping our hair looking decent afterwards. If you are like me, you are sweating like crazy within the first 20 minutes of exercise. So in addition to tricks like smoothing on Healthier Hair in a Bottle! Oil Spray and pulling my hair up in a high pony-tail where the ends don't touch my back or neck or putting my hair in two plaits (parted down the middle) while I work out and until the hair dries, I have come up with a *lite* conditioning rinse routine that can be used when those efforts fail. *Sometimes you just gotta get the sweat out and start over!* However, since you may have already shampooed your hair once or twice during the week (i.e., Weeks 1-6 or the Mid-Week/Refresher shampoo), this is more of a *conditioning rinse* than an actual shampoo. *It is not meant to replace your weekly shampooing and conditioning regimen (i.e., Weeks 1-6)*, but it can replace your Mid-Week/Refresher shampoo if you don't feel comfortable shampooing more than once a week. Regardless, this rinse can help our hair endure tough sweaty workouts during the week, allowing it to still look cute while we get into shape.

Because everyone sweats differently, *some women may not need this type of routine at all.* Some ladies can get their hair to look decent after a workout and wait until their regular weekly or mid-week refresher shampoo. To be honest, in most cases, *that would be me*, but then again I am lazy, and brisk walking is about the only activity I do consistently. So I have to say I very rarely use this routine. However, many women complain that the sweat and salt resulting from exercise wreaks the type of havoc their hair cannot bounce back from without water. So this mini-regimen is mainly for them, as well as for a growing group of women who prefer not to shampoo at all or who don't want to actually use shampoo more than once a week. Personally, I find this mini-regimen extremely useful if I *need to add moisture to my hair a few days before getting a touch-up.* I know many stylists tell you never to shampoo right before a touch-up, but in the Relaxing with Care chapter I talk about the dangers of getting chemical procedures done when our hair is overly dry or dehydrated (e.g., breakage, "shedding in the bowl", etc.). So to avoid this, if my hair feels dry, I do a conditioning *rinse* 3 or 4 days before my touch-up so that my hair still looks decent while I wait and is well moisturized as I see my stylist for a touch-up. Try the following steps to see if a conditioning rinse can help you too:

Shampooing & Conditioning Steps

1. **Rinse** your hair thoroughly with warm water, and **smooth** on a small amount of one of your favorite *crème* conditioners. Although you can certainly select the conditioner you prefer, I would not use an oil-based conditioner (e.g., hot oil treatments, etc.) because they can be hard to rinse out. I use one of the following: **Fantasia Aloe/Vitamin Anti-Breakage Formula Deep Penetrating Crème Moisturizer For Extra Dry Hair & Scalp; Motions Critical Protection & Repair; Organic Root Stimulator Hair Mayonnaise Treatment for Damaged Hair; KeraCare Humecto Crème Conditioner;** or **Ensure Acidifying Conditioner & Detangler.** Whichever one you choose, apply it to individual sections of your hair (I usually do at least 4 to 6 sections), from roots to ends, concentrating on the ends and *avoiding the scalp.* As a final step, smooth some on the top layer of your hair. You don't need to rub or scrub the scalp, but you will want to make sure the conditioner is evenly distributed. Leave it on for a few minutes (I do this in the shower, so I leave it on while I get cleaned up). You can put on a shower cap, twist your hair into a bun or just pull it back so that the conditioner is not washed off before you want it to be.

2. **Rinse** hair thoroughly. Start with warm water, but do your final rinse with cool water. Then gently **towel dry**.

3. **Apply** your favorite leave-in treatment(s) to your hair. I use **Healthier Hair in a Bottle! Moisturizing & Detangling Mist** and **Nu Expressions Moisturizing Foam Wrapping Lotion** by Bronner Brothers. I also just started using **Roux Fanci-Full Temporary Hair Color Rinse** (Formula 12 Black Rage) to cover my gray. For each of the products applied, let the length of your hair determine the amount you use. There is no need to saturate your hair with any of these products. Distribute them evenly, and **do not rinse**.

   IMPORTANT NOTE: If you plan to dry your hair by wrapping, roller, spiral or straw setting, you may want to substitute the setting lotion of your choice (e.g., Lottabody Texturizing Setting Lotion, Nu Expressions Moisturizing Foam Wrapping Lotion, Salon Finish For Silky Hair Foam Wrap & Style Lotion, etc.) for one or more of your leave-in treatments.

4. Gently **comb** through hair with a wide-tooth comb. Start at the ends and gently detangle, working from the ends to the root. Never comb hair from the roots to the ends without detangling first. Your hair is very fragile when it is wet, so handle it with care. Also, do not brush hair to remove tangles. Part the hair into 4 to 6 sections, and clip each section after combing, if necessary.

5. Go to Chapter 4 for tips on various drying methods (e.g., air drying, wet sets, etc.). If I do this routine at night, I usually do a twist set with a part down the middle, and twist the sections on each side, and then pin them.

SWIMMER'S HAIR THERAPY
(Chlorine Can't Mess with This!)

For far too long many of us have been held down by the fear of water's *evil effects* on our hair! I remember running when it rained, being told not to get my hair wet if I played in water and not really being interested in learning to swim because the idea of maintaining my hair was just too much to handle on a regular basis (that and the fact that I was chicken). I did not want the headache of having to shampoo my hair, blow dry it, and then hot curl it for 30 minutes or more to get it to look like something! As a result, I didn't even really learn how to swim until I was in my 30's. I tell you having kids will definitely make you face and conquer your fears!

I taught myself to do the *pitiful* swimming I can do during a week's vacation at the beach, which is also where I devised a plan to help keep my hair looking good, *not just decent*, during a time where I swam at least 5 days out of 7. Can you believe that I did not have a *blow dryer, hooded dryer, flat iron or a curling iron?* All I had was relatively clean hair that had been deep conditioned *before* the vacation (as described in any of the Weeks 1-6), shampoos, conditioners, leave-in treatments, a few scrunchies, a wide-tooth comb, a soft boar bristle brush, a hair clip, and bobby pins. I lived on plait and twist sets, air drying, and on some days, I just let it hang after combing through it, and let the wave pattern that God gave me try to peep through. This was usually the case if I did the *unthinkable*, swim twice in one day! My head is way too big for a swim cap – my hair would be broken off just trying to get the thing on, **and you know you have to wash the chlorine out EACH time!** However, as long as your hair is well moisturized, shiny and healthy-looking, you can get away with styles you never thought about wearing. Without wanting to sound corny, I have to say that this whole swimming experience literally changed my life – the way I view shampooing and maintaining my hair without a lot of fuss. I am beginning to think that *maybe we have been making it too hard on ourselves…*

After a few vacations over the years to practice this, I have gotten even bolder, I now will swim at night and wash my hair whenever – 9:00, 10:00, 11:00 or 12:00 (*I have not gotten any head colds as a result either*). It does not really matter anymore – *the regimen stays the same.* Shampoo and deep condition at least once a week as you normally would (e.g., as in Weeks 1-6), but for any other day that you swim during the week, try the following:

Shampooing & Conditioning Steps

1. *Before swimming,* section your hair and **smooth** on a little water (optional) and a small amount of **ION Anti-Chlorine Swimmer's Conditioner** or **Ion Hard Water Conditioner** on the hair from roots to ends, avoiding the scalp and *really focusing on the ends.* **Note:** *If you can't find one of these products, in a pinch, you could use a small amount of one of your other crème conditioners or a leave-in treatment like Infusium 23.* After that, I usually put it in one or two plaits – you could also do a few braids or cornrows. Because my hair usually comes loose pretty quickly, I started using a "Ouchless" headband by Goody as a pony-tail holder (wrapped around about 4 times) to keep my hair from getting tangled in my goggle straps. I thought this might work better than a fabric pony-tail holder. Regardless of how you choose to wear it, the point is to keep the hair out of your face while you are swimming. Ladies with shorter lengths may not have to worry about this problem, *but you still need to put a conditioner on before swimming.*

2. *After swimming,* **rinse** hair thoroughly with warm water for a few minutes to help remove chlorine and to help the shampoo lather more easily.

3. **Shampoo** hair with a cap full of **ION Anti-Chlorine Swimmer's Shampoo.** Because this shampoo is designed to remove chlorine from your hair, it can sometimes leave your hair feeling a little matted/tangled afterwards. To avoid this and make sure I remove all of the chlorine, I **lather a second time** with a different shampoo (e.g., choose from any of the ones you use in your weekly regimen). I might use about one capful (only as much as is needed) of either **Crème of Nature Ultra Moisturizing Formula for Dry, Brittle or Color-Treated Hair Detangling Conditioning Shampoo; KeraCare Hydrating Detangling Shampoo; Roux Porosity Control Shampoo; Aveda Sap Moss Shampoo**; or **Aubrey Organics Island Naturals Island Butter Shampoo.** If I am at home, I sometimes mix in a drop of an oil like almond, jojoba or rosehip (almond is cheaper and gets the job done) in the cap with the shampoo (I use a bobby pin to stir it, in case you are wondering).

4. **Rinse** hair thoroughly, and gently remove excess water.

5. Only do this step if you *have not* done your weekly deep conditioning as described in Weeks 1-6. **If you have already deep conditioned,** *go to step 7, skipping this step and step 6 below.* Otherwise, **apply ION Anti-Chlorine Swimmer's Conditioner** from the roots to the ends, focusing on the ends and avoiding the scalp. Then **apply** one of your favorite crème conditioners. I use **one** of the following: **Fantasia's Aloe/Vitamin Anti-Breakage Formula Deep Penetrating Crème Moisturizer For Extra Dry Hair & Scalp; Motions CPR; Organic Root Stimulator Hair Mayonnaise Treatment for Damaged Hair; KeraCare Humecto Crème Conditioner; Ensure Acidifying Conditioner & Detangler;** or **Aveda Sap Moss Conditioning Detangler** on top of the ION conditioner.

6. **Cover hair** with a plastic cap, and sit either under a dryer or a heating cap for at least 15 to 30 minutes, depending on the condition and texture of your hair. The conditioners are heat-activated. Therefore, the longer heat is applied, the more conditioning your hair receives. For those with fine hair or hair that is not damaged or subjected to constant heat styling and abuse, 10-15 minutes may be sufficient. However, if more conditioning is needed, increase the time spent under the heating cap or dryer accordingly. Because my hair is coarse and prone to dryness, I try to stay under my dryer for at least 30 minutes; and the benefits are phenomenal! You can decide how long you apply heat, but for people with dryness, breakage or damaged hair, this step is critical. WARNING: *Please be sure to follow ALL of the manufacturer's instructions for your heating cap or dryer.* There may be special warnings for people with certain illnesses or conditions (e.g., diabetes or circulatory problems). **Go to step 8.**

7. *Skip this step if you did steps 5 & 6 above.* Otherwise, if you *have* already done your weekly deep conditioning as described in Weeks 1-6, you don't have to deep condition, meaning you can **do a light conditioning treatment while in the shower**. For light conditioning, **smooth** on some **ION Anti-Chlorine Swimmer's Conditioner** from the roots to the ends, focusing on the ends, and avoiding the scalp. Leave it on for a few minutes while getting cleaned up. **If you feel the need for extra conditioning** (I usually do), after rinsing you could also **smooth on** one of your favorite crème conditioners. I use **one** of the following: **Fantasia's Aloe/Vitamin Anti-Breakage Formula Deep Penetrating Crème Moisturizer For Extra Dry Hair & Scalp; Motions CPR; Organic Root Stimulator Hair Mayonnaise Treatment for Damaged Hair; KeraCare Humecto Crème Conditioner; Roux Porosity Control pH 4.5 Corrector & Conditioner**; or **Ensure Acidifying Conditioner & Detangler**. Pay special attention to your ends, and leave it on for a few minutes as you continue showering. You can twist your hair into a bun, or just pull it back so that the conditioner is not washed off before you want it to be.

8. **Rinse** hair thoroughly, first with warm water and finally with cool water. Then, gently towel hair dry.

9. **Spray** your hair with the leave-in treatment(s) *of your choice* or pour a small amount into your hands/hair and work through. I use **Healthier Hair in a Bottle! Moisturizing & Detangling Mist** and **Nu Expressions Moisturizing Foam Wrapping Lotion** by Bronner Brothers. I also just started using **Roux Fanci-Full Temporary Hair Color Rinse** (Formula 12 Black Rage) to cover my gray. For each of the products applied, let the length of your hair determine the amount you use. There is no need to saturate your hair with any of these products. Distribute them evenly, and **do not rinse**.

   IMPORTANT NOTE: If you plan to dry your hair by wrapping, roller, spiral or straw setting, substitute the setting lotion of your choice (e.g., Lottabody Texturizing Setting Lotion, Nu Expressions Moisturizing Foam Wrapping Lotion, Salon Finish For Silky Hair Foam Wrap & Style Lotion, etc.) for one or more of your leave-in treatments.

10. Gently **comb** through hair with a wide-tooth comb. Start at the ends and gently detangle, working from the ends to the root. Never comb hair from the roots to the ends without detangling first. Your hair is very fragile when it is wet, so handle it with care. Also, do not brush hair to remove tangles. Part the hair into 4 to 6 sections, and clip each section after combing.

11. Go to Chapter 4 for tips on various drying methods (e.g., air drying, wet sets, etc.). If I do this routine at night or during the day while I am on vacation, I usually do a twist set with a part down the middle (I twist the sections on each side and pin them) or a plait set with one plait in the back.

Helpful Alternatives/Tips:

- *What if you cannot complete all of the steps (1-11) immediately? Say you have to run errands right after swimming (e.g., pick up kids, shop, etc.), or you are want to go from the pool to the beach to hang out with friends, or you are sticking around for a pool party? This is why it has taken me so long to finish this edition of the book – I keep thinking of new things!!! I recently took my boys swimming, and they insisted I swim too. I said cool, we played and I swam, so then I was ready to head home and go through steps 1-11, above. Well, right as I was leaving some neighbors asked us to meet them at the gym in 45 minutes (the adults would work out, and the kids would play). Of course the kids were excited, but I was thinking how do I make dinner for the kids, do my hair, get changed, and drive to the gym in 45 minutes? Not to mention doing all that work only to sweat and take another shower immediately after! Usually I would have just said no, but I tend to get suckered when my boys are involved. As a result of this situation, while making dinner, I decided to rinse my hair and do a quick shampoo with the **ION Anti-Chlorine Shampoo** before going to the gym. After squeezing out the excess water, I worked some **Aveda Sap Moss Nourishing Concentrate Pre-Shampoo Healing Treatment for Dry Hair** (you could also try a hot oil treatment like **Healthier Hair in a Bottle! Hot Oil Treatment**) through it, paying special attention to the ends. I then slicked it back into a pony-tail and wrapped the hair around the base of it, securing it with bobby pins. It was actually cute and very slick looking! I did my work out, and at about two hours after swimming, I shampooed with **Aveda Sap Moss Shampoo** and conditioned (while in the shower) with **Aveda Sap Moss Conditioning Detangler**. From there I picked up at step 9. I have to say that this was the silkiest my hair has ever felt after swimming. So maybe on one of your busy/crazy days that you want to get a swim in, this might be a worthwhile tip to try.*

- *I was a chaperone on a pool field trip this past summer and I saw a young woman wearing braids. She had them pinned up, but she also had a silk scarf wrapped around the front and middle. Since she was near an area where I was watching children, I noticed that she was being very careful not to get her hair wet even though she was in the pool – she mainly caught my attention because she did not look like she was having a good time. Watching her made me wonder how easy/difficult it is for braid/extension braid wearers to get chlorine out of braided hair. As I thought about it, I could understand that it might not be as easy as it is for a person wearing their hair loose. So a thought came to me, I know it is probably crazy, but I thought I would share it anyway. What if a person with braided hair filled a sink with warm water and splashed a little shampoo (e.g., Ion, Crème of Nature, Aubrey Organics, etc.) in it to create light suds and submerged the braids and scalp in it for a few minutes. I would say only long enough to let the braids become saturated and to get them rinsed thoroughly. I would think one or two dips in the sink ought to do it. However, no heavy rubbing should be done; otherwise, braids might become undone or start to fray. After cleaning this way, you could just run clean water onto the braids while in the sink or shower, or you could fill the sink with clean water, splash a little conditioner in (e.g., Ion, KeraCare, etc.) and dip your hair again. Then do a final rinse in the sink or shower – if you go the sink route, how would a diluted leave-in treatment sound? Not being a braid wearer or an expert on the subject, it sounds crazy enough to work. If you try it, I would love to hear the results.*

SEVERELY DRY HAIR TREATMENT

If you have a dry hair condition that has not improved as much as you would like by following the shampooing and conditioning regimens described in the previous sections **and** you know that there is nothing that you are doing to contribute to it (e.g., frequent heat styling, overprocessing, etc.) **and** you have ruled out any medical conditions then *this last resort routine may be the treatment for you*. My hair can get pretty dry sometimes, especially as I pass the 7th and 8th weeks of a relaxer. In the past, some of this could have been related to poor diet (e.g., vitamin or mineral deficiencies), anemia, a dry heating system, inconsistent or inadequate moisturizing. I am not sure if there is a sole culprit – it is really hard to tell since I have always had really dry skin too. Shampooing every 3-4 days helps me keep it under control though, but every once in a while, I like to give my hair an extra moisture boost. By now, I am sure many of you may have seen advertisements for Aveda's Sap Moss products. I know they can be a little pricey (I have seen some salons that sell samples), but they work wonders for an "every-once-in-a-while" or "as needed treatment". Everyone's hair may not need something this intensive, but for those of you who might, you can give this a try:

Shampooing & Conditioning Steps:

1. **Apply Aveda Sap Moss Nourishing Concentrate Pre-Shampoo Healing Treatment for Dry Hair** to *damp* hair, from the roots to the ends. Leave it on for at least 1-2 minutes. *I have left it on for as long as a few hours, but you can check out the directions to decide how long you should leave it on.*

2. **Rinse** hair thoroughly with warm water, and **shampoo** with a very small amount of **Aveda Sap Moss Shampoo**. This shampoo does not produce a traditional foamy, white lather, but if you part your hair in sections, and massage a little shampoo into one section at a time, while making sure each section is very wet before applying the shampoo, it will lather better. One lather should be enough. Rinse hair, and gently towel dry.

3. **Apply Aveda Sap Moss Conditioning Detangler.** For extra conditioning, you could also apply **Fantasia's Aloe/Vitamin Anti-Breakage Formula Deep Penetrating Crème Moisturizer For Extra Dry Hair & Scalp** on top (*this is optional*). Work the conditioner(s) evenly through the hair, from roots to ends, avoiding the scalp and concentrating on the ends. Leave it on for a few minutes before rinsing. There is no need to sit under a dryer or heating cap for this treatment *unless you want to*. Because I tend to do this in the shower, I usually leave the conditioner on while I get cleaned up. Then as I am rinsing off, I rinse the conditioner off too.

4. **Rinse** hair thoroughly, first with warm water and finally with cool water. Then, gently towel hair dry.

5. **Apply** your favorite leave-in treatment(s) to your hair. I use **Healthier Hair in a Bottle! Moisturizing & Detangling Mist** and **Nu Expressions Moisturizing Foam Wrapping Lotion** by Bronner Brothers. I also just started using **Roux Fanci-Full Temporary Hair Color Rinse** (Formula 12 Black Rage) to cover my

gray. For each of the products applied, let the length of your hair determine the amount you use. There is no need to saturate your hair with any of these products. Distribute them evenly, and **do not rinse**.

IMPORTANT NOTE: If you plan to dry your hair by wrapping, roller, spiral or straw setting, you may want to substitute the setting lotion of your choice (e.g., Lottabody Texturizing Setting Lotion, Nu Expressions Moisturizing Foam Wrapping Lotion, Salon Finish For Silky Hair Foam Wrap & Style Lotion, etc.) for one or more of your leave-in treatments.

6. Gently **comb** through hair with a wide-tooth comb. Start at the ends and gently detangle, working from the ends to the root. Never comb hair from the roots to the ends without detangling first. Your hair is very fragile when it is wet, so handle it with care. Also, do not brush hair to remove tangles. Part the hair into 4 to 6 sections, and clip each section after combing, if necessary.

7. Go to Chapter 4 for tips on various drying methods (e.g., air drying, wet sets, etc.).

Chapter 4

Drying Methods

Now that your hair is shampooed and conditioned, what do you do now to continue on in your new healthier hair care regimen? Well, even though many of us realize that a consistent shampooing and conditioning regimen is essential for healthy hair, it may not be as obvious that the way we dry our hair *afterwards* is enough to make or break that regimen. For years I compared my hair to my cousin Rosalind's, and I wondered why her hair was so much healthier and *longer* than mine? Could it have been the fact that I never deep conditioned my hair when I washed it at home and then blow dried it *every* time I shampooed; whereas, at the time, she usually had her hair shampooed, conditioned and set by her stylist? Her hair was beautiful then, and it still is even as she maintains it at home for the most part now. I have to admit that I learn so much in life by watching people who have or are doing something that I aspire to, and this area was no exception. Watching my cousin and other women with beautiful hair first caused me to want the kind of hair they had, and then it made me want to find out what I could do to get my hair to look like theirs! This book is a way for me to share some of what I learned.

One of my many "light bulb" moments regarding why my hair length seemed to have reached a plateau (right at shoulder level) and why I was plagued with split-ends happened as I whined, yet again, to my cousin about the state of my hair. I think I must have mentioned that I had just finished blow drying my hair, and she *innocently* stated that she did not blow dry her hair on a regular basis. Although she didn't say it in a mean way, *the way* she said it made me think that there could be something wrong with this being my primary way of drying my hair. I was using my blow dryer with the comb attachment every time I shampooed, and sometimes I even let my stylist blow dry it if either of us was in a hurry. Could there really be something wrong with blow drying relaxed hair on a regular basis? I didn't know, but I set out on a mission to find out.

In that search, one of the most enlightening articles I read was in *Try It Yourself Hair* magazine (April 1998) called "Hair Facts, The Heat is On." This article provided the following information from Helene Curtis Research that tells how hot our "heat styling" can really get:

The average temperature of heat appliances is 250°:

Hair Dryer	=	250°
Curling Iron	=	290°
Hot Curlers	=	220°

According to research from the same study, "Heat temporarily changes the protein structure of hair, making it susceptible to damage." The study also found that 50% of all hair fibers that come in contact with heat appliances become damaged. I did not realize that much of the breakage I used to experience resulted from blow drying my sopping wet hair with a comb attachment (not even wide-toothed) on the highest setting until it was completely dry. Back then I did not see a problem with this – I didn't realize that our hair is most vulnerable when it is wet. So pulling a comb attachment through our wet hair while a stream of hot air over 200° blows on it is **not** something we should be doing on a regular basis! Natural sisters obviously have more flexibility, especially if their hair is virgin. However, for the most part, the lesson I have learned is that we should find a variety of ways to dry our hair so that we *minimize our hair's exposure to **direct heat** and **stress** (pulling, combing & brushing) as much as possible.*

One of the first alternatives that comes to mind for relaxed hair is a hooded/bonnet dryer, which is a healthy exception because: 1) It does not expose our ends to direct heat; 2) it does not involve pulling or combing individual strands of hair; and 3) it provides sets that can last at least a week, which reduces the overall amount of heat styling required. I will talk more about wet sets later, but for some of us who are not proficient in setting our own hair and do not want to go to a stylist on a regular basis, even more alternatives are needed. As a result, in my first book, I shared the *air drying* methods I came up with for relaxed hair. I have continued to do this over the years, and I have come up with ways to make it even simpler for anyone who may have struggled to perfect it in the past. There are also plait, twist and braid sets that can be done by sisters with natural and relaxed hair. I think that if we are creative and learn to appreciate our hair's own natural curl pattern, we can come up with all sorts of different drying methods and styles that can help us have the healthy hair we want. We just need to open our minds a bit... Now that our minds are open, let's talk about my favorite drying method.

AIR DRYING

Air drying is a term that simply means drying your hair without the use of heat appliances (e.g., blow dryers, hooded dryers, etc.). Although I came up with a few variations of it **mainly for relaxed hair**, it *can be used for ladies or girls with natural hair as well, depending on the hair type and the style you are trying to create.* After finding an air drying method that worked for me, **I threw away my blow dryer**, and *I have not owned one since.* I knew that owning one was not good for me because in a pinch, **I would use it**! As a result, I was forced to make this *air drying thing* work. Obviously, there was a *withdrawal phase*, but after a while, I found a method I could do relatively easily and still get the results I wanted. As a result, for the past 7 years, *I have air dried my hair every time I shampoo it myself,* which aside from the few times a year that I have a touch-up, is all the time. Believe it or not, *I am able to get my hair as straight as if I blow dried it* even as late as 11 or 12 weeks into my relaxer. Of course the roots may be wavy because of new growth, but *the ends are straight.* Some of you may have seen pictures posted on my website showing me air drying at different points in my relaxer.

This technique is perfect for days when you are working around the house or running errands. Instead of being in a hair salon for hours, you can get important tasks accomplished (e.g., cooking, cleaning, shopping, playing with your kids or working). This option gives you a lot of freedom and flexibility especially if you swim or work out, and this is what I do after completing the shampooing and conditioning regimen in Weeks 1-6. Here are instructions for air drying hair of all lengths:

1. Complete one of the shampooing and conditioning regimens in Chapter 3 (e.g., Week 1, Mid-Week/ Refresher, Swimmer's Hair Therapy, etc.).
2. Continue combing (use a very wide-tooth comb) through your favorite leave-in treatments and detangling your hair until it is relatively tangle-free and flat.
3. Part your hair in small sections, and oil your scalp with a very rich oil like **Healthier Hair in a Bottle! Oil Spray** (I used to use Wild Growth Hair Oil). After parting a section, I spray a few squirts onto my scalp, and rub it in. Before going to the next section, I rub a small amount of oil between my hands and rub it on the hair, especially the ends. When done, smooth any oil left on your hands on your edges and ends. *Make sure ends are well covered.*

From there, choose from the following methods based on the results you are trying to achieve and your hair type and length:

If your hair is long enough to be pulled into a pony-tail and you want to dry it STRAIGHT try...

The Pony-Tail Method

1. Have a scrunchie, coated hair band, bow or clip handy, and **gently comb hair back** into one or more sections, making sure that the hair is *tangle-free* and lays as flat as possible. *This is very important! If your hair is not flat when it is wet, it will not be flat and straight at the root when it dries!*
2. Before securing the hair in a pony-tail, **smooth** it with your hands **from front to ends**. A little more oil may be used, as needed, in this smoothing process – it depends on your hair type, density, and the type of oil used. This process helps to keep ends from frizzing and seals in moisture so that your hair dries with sheen.
3. **Secure hair** (not too tightly, but firmly). Once hair is pulled back securely, smooth it with your hands or a very soft boar-bristled brush from the front of the hair to the base of the scrunchie/bow/clip to make sure hair is flat and there are no fly-aways. For hair that cannot be securely pulled into a pony-tail because of its length or the way it is cut, try moving the pony-tail up from the nape of your neck towards the center of the head. The higher up the pony-tail is, the easier it may be to include all of the ends. However, if you are still unable to include all of the hair securely, you can smooth the fly-away strands down or you can try the next variation of this method.
4. **Give** the ends hanging from the pony-tail **one final comb-through** to minimize frizz.
5. **Apply** a final coating of **Healthier Hair in a Bottle! Oil Spray** (I spray a very small amount of it in my hands, rub them together, and smooth it on) to the pony-tail and to the hair leading up to it. In the past, I have also rubbed on a little **Fantasia Hair Polisher** afterwards to prevent frizz. However, more recently, I have not needed it, so I very rarely use it. *I am only mentioning it for people who have asked me in the past how to minimize frizz, and this is one of the ways.*
6. Although it is optional, **moisturize the ends** of the pony-tail with a little **Healthier Hair in a Bottle! Ends Treatment**. Before developing this product, I used to use a little **Vaseline**. I am only talking about a small dab rubbed between your fingers and applied to the bottom ½ inch of the pony-tail. This is done mainly to protect the ends from breakage and frizzing, but it also helps them to dry even straighter.
7. As the hair dries over the next few hours, **comb** it through at least two times *before* it dries completely. You can also smooth on more **Healthier Hair in a Bottle! Oil Spray** as needed, but **use it sparingly** so your hair does not become oily. When your hair is dry, *it should feel moisturized, not greasy or oily.* After each comb-through, put it back in the pony-tail until it is completely dry.
8. Once the top layer of hair is dry, you may **quicken the drying process** by removing the bow and letting your hair hang loose – a form of air drying which should work because your roots have already begun to dry straight. Gently comb through as needed. I use this method a lot, and my hair still dries as straight as it would if I blow dried it. Trust me, you will be amazed at how well this works on relaxed hair!
9. **Style as desired**, and spray hair lightly with **Isoplus Oil Sheen Hair Spray** or **Jheri Redding Volumizer Extra Shine** *Spray-On-Shine* for added sheen. *This is optional.*

Quick Tip: If you are at the beach, you can get a quick and simple wavy look, by plaiting or braiding the damp pony-tail. When it dries, you can wear the hair hanging loose or pulled up in various styles. This helps me to avoid bad hair days at the beach, especially when I am in the later weeks of my relaxer.

If your hair is NOT long enough to be pulled into a pony-tail and you want to dry it **STRAIGHT** *try…*

The Slicked-Backed Method (*also works for medium and long hair*)

1. If your hair is too short or too uneven to pull it securely into a pony-tail(s), **gently comb** it to the back of your head as if to put it into one or more pony-tails. Slick the hair back, using a comb and your hands, until it lays flat and smoothly rests at the nape of your neck. *This is very important! If your hair is not flat when it is wet, it won't be flat when it dries!*

2. **Spray** a small amount of **Healthier Hair in a Bottle! Oil Spray** in your hands, rub them together, and **smooth** another coating on the hair from the front to the ends, making sure your ends are well coated. This will keep ends from frizzing and seal in moisture so that your hair dries with sheen. In the past, I have also rubbed on a little **Fantasia Hair Polisher** afterwards to prevent frizz. However, more recently, I have not needed it, so I very rarely use it. *I am only mentioning it for people who have asked me in the past how to minimize frizz, and this is one of the ways.*

Quick Tip: *If you are feeling adventurous, this would be a great time to try John Frieda's Frizz-Ease Relax for Chemically-Straightened Hair Ripple Effect Wave-Maker Styling Spray (and I thought Healthier Hair in a Bottle was a long name!). Although the product's directions say to just use the spray on wet hair and does not suggest that you use other leave-in treatments or oil on your scalp and hair, I got pretty decent results using it in this air drying routine. I sprayed the product on my hair after following the steps at the beginning of this section and scrunched sections of the hair as directed while it air dried. I did not use a blow dryer or diffuser attachment as they suggested. I scrunched it with my hands as I went about my normal activities. I also twisted or plaited large sections of my hair as it dried to make the curls more pronounced. This is something I would do during the summer, especially at the beach. Can you picture yourself at the beach, in a sun dress with loose flowing curls (short or long), acting like someone with naturally curly hair? I say it is definitely worth a try. If you can find a style that works for you using this product, imagine how much time you could save on styling, and how much heat damage you could prevent. If you are nervous about trying it, do it at a time when you have nothing to lose, say you are on vacation and you plan to swim or plan to be in the house for a while. Worst case scenario: pull or pin the hair back until you shampoo again.*

However, if you are not feeling adventurous, continue on with the next air drying step below…

3. Either use a clip or bobby pins to **keep hair firmly resting at the nape of your neck** or leave it loose, and periodically **smooth it down** with your hands or a soft boar-bristle brush.

4. Although it is *optional*, I **moisturize** my **ends** with a little **Healthier Hair in a Bottle! Ends Treatment**. Before developing this product, I used to use a little **Vaseline**. I am only talking about a small dab rubbed between your fingers and applied to the bottom ½ inch of the hair. This is done mainly to protect the ends from breakage and frizzing, but it also helps them to dry even straighter.

5. As the hair dries over the next few hours, **comb** it through at least two times *before* it dries completely. You can also smooth on more **Healthier Hair in a Bottle! Oil Spray** as needed, but **use it sparingly** so your hair does not become oily. When your hair is dry, *it should feel moisturized, not greasy or oily.* After each comb-through, you can leave the hair loose or re-clip it until it is completely dry.

6. Style as desired, and spray hair lightly with **Isoplus Oil Sheen Hair Spray** or **Jheri Redding Volumizer Extra Shine** *Spray-On-Shine* for added sheen. *This is optional.*

If you want to dry it STRAIGHT regardless of hair length, but also want body and bounce try...

The Wrap Set

Note: *If you have never "wrapped" hair, you might want to get your stylist or a friend to demonstrate the technique using your hair or someone else's, to help you get the hang of it. There are so many variations that a stylist would be the best person to recommend the best one for your hair and face. The directions shown below demonstrate a **very basic wrap** and will make more sense if you already have an idea of how a wrap is done.*

1. Decide which direction you want your hair to hang or fall. Then **make a part** on the opposite side of your head **in the front**. You are going to wrap the hair in the opposite direction of the way you want it to hang or fall.
2. **Smooth hair** in the direction opposite of the direction you want it to hang or fall. Use a wide-tooth comb to **gently comb/smooth** the hair from the side of the part towards the back of the neck. Continue smoothing until the hair lays flat. Make sure the length of your hair has been smoothed over as far as it can go (for medium and shoulder length hair, that is resting on your opposite shoulder).
3. Next **part** a small, diagonal section starting from the part in the front of your hair. **While holding the palm of your hand on the top of your head** *(very important* – to keep the loose hair from being pulled with the section you are wrapping), comb this section around the already wrapped hair that is resting at the base of your neck. Use a comb to gently rake the hair until it rests flat and smooth on top of the already wrapped hair.
4. Repeat step 3 until only a small section of hair is left (only the hair resting at the base of your neck should remain). After wrapping a couple of sections, gently smooth or **tighten the wrap** with your hands or a comb.
5. **Comb** the remaining section around the already wrapped hair. Use your hands or a comb to **smooth and tighten the wrap**. You can smooth on a little oil like **Healthier Hair in a Bottle! Oil Spray**, if you like.
6. Place bobby pins in front and/or behind both ears to keep the wrap in place.
7. Let the hair **dry** as you walk around the house or overnight as you sleep. However, if you do it overnight, you may want to cover it with a silk/satin scarf to keep the wrap in place.
8. When dry, **gently unwrap hair**, using your fingers and/or a brush to smooth.
9. Style as desired, and spray hair lightly with **Isoplus Oil Sheen Hair Spray** or **Jheri Redding Volumizer Extra Shine** *Spray-On-Shine* for added sheen. *This is optional.*

If you want to dry it with crimp-like curls, whether your hair is long or short try...

The Plait or Braid Set

1. **Part** hair into one or more sections, smaller or larger depending on how tight or long-lasting you want the crimp/curl to be. Basically, do as many as you feel like plaiting/braiding. The smaller the sections, the fuller the style will be. You can even do one.
2. Starting with one section at a time, **separate** the hair into three strands, **plait/braid** hair from the scalp to the ends. **Continue plaiting/braiding** sections until your entire head is plaited/braided.
3. Let hair **dry** as you go about your normal day or overnight while you sleep.
4. When dry or almost dry, **loosen** or undo the plaits/braids.
5. **Separate** each section with your fingers, smoothing on **Healthier Hair in a Bottle! Oil Spray** as needed, and finger-comb. Do not use a comb unless you want to loosen the curls. *Keep in mind, that it may not look like much until all of the sections are separated and finger-combed.*
6. After all of the sections are separated, style as desired, and spray hair lightly with **Isoplus Oil Sheen Hair Spray** or **Jheri Redding Volumizer Extra Shine** *Spray-On-Shine* if you want more sheen. *This is optional.*

If you want to dry it with wavy, spiral-like curls, whether your hair is long or short try...

The Twist Set

1. **Part** hair into one or more sections, smaller or larger depending on how tight you want the curls to be. The smaller the sections, the fuller the style. I usually do two to five, but I have also done just one.
2. **Twist** hair from the scalp to the ends for each section. Once firmly twisted, take the end and wrap it completely around the base of the section (at the scalp), tucking the end of the hair under the wrapped hair. Use a bobby pin(s) to **secure each section**, if needed.
3. Let hair **dry** as you go about your normal day or overnight while you sleep.
4. When the hair is dry or almost dry, **remove** the pins and **untwist** sections. I usually do this when my hair is at least 75% dry, and as long as you smooth on a little oil (e.g., Healthier Hair in a Bottle! Oil Spray, etc.), there should not be a problem with frizz.
5. **Separate each section** with your fingers, smoothing on **Healthier Hair in a Bottle! Oil Spray** as needed, and finger-comb. Do not use a regular comb unless you want to loosen the curls. *Keep in mind, that it may not look like much until all of the sections are separated and finger-combed.*
6. After all of the sections are separated, **style as desired**, and **spray** hair lightly with **Isoplus Oil Sheen Hair Spray** or **Jheri Redding Volumizer Extra Shine** *Spray-On-Shine* if you want more sheen. *This is optional.*

General Air Drying Tips

- For anyone whose hair tends to frizz, try smoothing on a silicon-based product such as **Fantasia IC Hair Polisher** or **John Frieda's Frizz-Ease Serum**. I have found these extremely helpful, especially for the ends.

- As your hair is drying, be sure to use a paper towel or tissue to wipe any traces of oil from your edges, face or neck. Because the oil *may run,* make sure you do a spot check before you leave the house, and **bring something with you to wipe just in case.**

- If you started off with your hair in a pony-tail, clipped, pinned or wrapped, and *you need to finish the drying process in a hurry,* you can speed things along by sitting under a dryer. You can also blow dry the loose hair (minus the comb/brush attachment), just *don't do this on a regular basis.* I admit that your hair will be a little sleeker, but *I don't do it* because of the risk of heat damage, and I don't mind going places with wet hair (*if memory serves me correctly, I have never gotten a head cold from doing this*). Sometimes I have even gone to Church with my hair wet. Usually it's just the roots, so I can still curl the ends.

- If you do choose to blow dry to speed up the drying process, let your hair air dry for a few hours first if you can – this will make blow drying a little less damaging, *especially if your hair is relaxed.*

- If you plan to do an overnight set, leave your hair parted down the middle, and let it air dry hanging straight until bedtime. Then put it in the desired set (e.g., two pony-tails, plaits or twists). This allows it to dry faster and more evenly. You could also sit under a hooded dryer with it hanging straight for about 10 minutes or so to get most of the moisture out, and then do your overnight set. Also, you could do the set of your choice (e.g., plait, braid or twists), and then sit under the hooded dryer for 15-20 minutes to partially dry it before going to bed. If you do this, make sure you use a rich oil on the hair and ends as well as on the scalp so you have a lot of sheen the next day.

- Although you *can* go to bed on wet hair and still air dry it straight, it does require extra care to get the same results. You must be careful not to sleep on the loose hair; otherwise, your ends may dry with a bend or wave, instead of being straight. Also, your roots may not dry straight if they are pushed up while you sleep. However, if you must go to sleep while your hair is still wet, you could part your hair down the middle and secure it with clips, pins or bows. I have done it many times by putting my hair in two pony-tails that hang on the side and sleeping on my back, with a towel on my pillow. Gently comb out the loose hair, and apply a little more **Healthier Hair in a Bottle! Oil Spray** if the hair appears dull. Make sure you do not sleep on the loose hair. Lying on the back is preferable, allowing the hair to loosely rest on the pillow.

- For twist sets, the smaller the sections, the greater chance there is for tangling. As a result, be very careful as you separate curls. Handle tangles with care by smoothing the tangled strands out as straight as they can go, and spray a small amount of **Healthier Hair in a Bottle! Moisturizing and Detangling Spray** or some other detangling leave-in treatment on it, and either separate it with your fingers, or comb it gently with a fine tooth comb. Be gentle – unresolved or roughly-treated tangles can mean breakage.

- If you air dried your hair in a straight style, you can go to the Styling section for tips on styling dry hair (e.g., curling or bumping with the Caruso Steam Hair Setter, etc.).

- Air drying really does work, it just takes a little practice.

Air Drying Pictures

Before:

After:

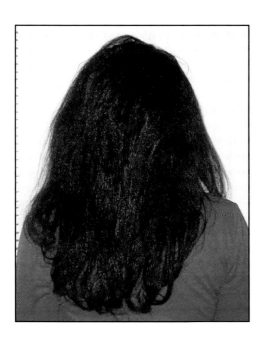

Less than perfect air drying after the Pony-tail method, but I was still able to wear this look to Church. My hair was not totally dry, but I could still curl the ends. Very little effort and heat!

At 6 weeks in my relaxer, I air dried using the Pony-tail method and curled the ends with Caruso curlers. It is obviously nothing fancy, but it works for me.

WET SETS

Wet sets, especially roller, rod or straw sets, are a favorite among many women I have talked to who have healthy hair – especially for those who go to the salon. Some of the sets are similar to the ones you saw in the Air Drying section; however, once the hair is set on rollers, braids, plaits, twists or a wrap, you sit under a hooded or bonnet dryer until your hair is completely dry. These types of sets offer some of the most flexible and long-lasting styles you can get, and because heat is involved, the styles tend to be a little sleeker and glossier than those done by air drying. If you go to a salon this would be a healthier alternative to having the stylist blow dry your hair and hot curl it.

Many women, myself included, find it hard to roll and clip their hair using magnetic curlers. *This is one of the main reasons I find myself air drying all the time.* However, as with anything else, practice can make perfect. After a few attempts, and some pointers from your stylist, you can become a roller-setting guru. However, in the meantime, I can offer a few general tips in this area.

1. Complete one of the shampooing and conditioning regimens in Chapter 3 (e.g., Week 1, Mid-Week/ Refresher, Swimmer's Hair Therapy, etc.).
2. Lightly spray your hair with your favorite setting/wrapping lotion (e.g., Nu Expressions Moisturizing Foam Wrapping Lotion, Lottabody WRAP 'N TAP 'N Wrapping Lotion & Conditioner, Salon Finish Foam, etc.). *To avoid hard, stiff or frizzy curls, you may want to dilute the setting lotion.*
3. Comb through using a very wide tooth comb and detangle your hair until it is relatively tangle-free and flat.

From there, choose from the following methods based on the results you are trying to achieve and your hair type and length:

If you want long-lasting, traditional curls that look like the ones you might get at the salon, whether your hair is long or short try...

Roller, Rod or Straw Sets

1. **Part hair** into 1-inch sections, can be larger or smaller depending on the curling pattern you choose and the style you want to create. However, to make the set last longer and the curls tighter, make smaller sections.
2. **Comb** each section with a close-toothed comb (e.g., rat-tail comb – no jagged edges though), and gently comb each section to make sure it is tangle-free.
3. **Roll** one section at a time onto a magnetic curler, rod (e.g., flexi, perm, etc.) or straw, and **clip or secure** the curler, rod or straw in place.
4. **Sit under hair dryer** until your hair is completely dry, the actual time depends on the length/thickness of your hair.
5. When hair is completely dry, **remove the rollers, rods** or **straws**.
6. **Style as desired** and spray hair lightly with **Isoplus Oil Sheen Hair Spray** or **Jheri Redding Volumizer Extra Shine** *Spray-On-Shine* for more sheen. *This is optional.*

If you have a fierce short cut, and you want something other than the traditional roller/rod/straw set, try...

Finger Waves or Pin Curl Sets

1. **Part hair** into 1-inch sections, can be larger or smaller depending on the curling pattern you choose and the style you want to create.
2. **Comb** each section with a close-toothed comb (e.g., rat-tail comb – no jagged edges though), and gently comb each section to make sure it is tangle-free.
3. Either **clamp** each section with a wave clip, and go to step 4, *OR* **hold** a section, and put your fingers on the mid-way point of each section, and use the comb to make a curl. Wrap the curl around your fingers, and wind the hair in a circle until you get to the scalp. Make sure the ends of each section are inside the curl/circle. Hold each curl, and **clip or secure** it in place with pins or clips.
4. **Sit under hair dryer** until your hair is completely dry, the actual time depends on the length/thickness of your hair.
5. When hair is completely dry, **remove the wave clips or pins**.
6. **Style as desired** and spray hair lightly with **Isoplus Oil Sheen Hair Spray** or **Jheri Redding Volumizer Extra Shine** *Spray-On-Shine* for more sheen. *This is optional*

If you want long-lasting, wavy, spiral-like curls that look like the ones sported by our sisters with naturally curly hair, whether your hair is long or short try...

The Twist Set

1. **Part hair** into equal sections, can be larger or smaller depending on the curling pattern you choose and the style you want to create. To make the set last longer and the waves tighter, make smaller sections.
2. **Twist** each section from the scalp to the end. Once firmly twisted, take the end and **wrap** it around the base of the section (at the scalp), **tucking the end** of the hair under the wrapped hair. Use bobby pins to **secure each twist**, as needed.
3. **Sit under hair dryer** until hair is completely dry, the actual time depends on the length/thickness of your hair.
4. When dry, **remove** the pins and **unwrap each section**. Then **separate** each twist *slowly and carefully* (this set has the greatest potential for tangles).
5. Then **finger-comb** and **style as desired**. Do not use a regular comb unless you want to loosen the curls. *Keep in mind, that it may not look like much until all of the sections are separated and finger-combed.* You can bump the ends if you like (see Styling section).
6. Spray your hair lightly with **Isoplus Oil Sheen Hair Spray** or **Jheri Redding Volumizer Extra Shine Spray-On-Shine** for added sheen. *This is optional*

If you want long-lasting, crimp-like curls, whether your hair is long or short try...

The Plait/Braid Set

1. **Part hair** into 1-inch sections, can be larger or smaller depending on the level of fullness you want to create. To make the set last longer and the crimps tighter, make smaller sections.
2. **Plait/Braid** each section from the scalp to the end. If you want the ends to curl under you can roll the ends on rods or magnetic curlers. However, to save time, I would just bump large sections during step 5 with curlers from the Caruso Steam Hair Setter (see the Styling section).
3. **Sit under hair dryer** until your hair is completely dry, the actual time depends on the length/thickness of your hair.
4. When your hair is dry, carefully **loosen** each plait or braid.
5. Then **finger-comb** and **style as desired**. Do not use a regular comb unless you want to loosen the curls. *Keep in mind, that it may not look like much until all of the sections are separated and finger-combed.*
6. Spray your hair lightly with **Isoplus Oil Sheen Hair Spray** or **Jheri Redding Volumizer Extra Shine Spray-On-Shine** for added sheen. *This is optional*

If you want a straight style with incredible bounce and swing, whether your hair is long or short try...

The Wrap Set

Note: *If you have never "wrapped" hair, you might want to get your stylist or a friend to demonstrate the technique using your hair or someone else's to help you get the hang of it. There are so many variations that a stylist would be the best person to recommend the right one for your hair and face. The directions shown below demonstrate a very basic wrap and will make more sense if you already have an idea of how a wrap is done.*

1. Decide which direction you want your hair to hang or fall. Then **make a part** on the opposite side of your head **in the front**. You are going to wrap the hair in the opposite direction of the way you want it to hang or fall.
2. **Smooth hair** in the direction opposite of the direction you want it to hang or fall. Use a wide-tooth comb to **gently comb/smooth** the hair from the side of the part towards the back of the neck. Continue smoothing until the hair lays flat. Make sure the length of your hair has been smoothed over as far as it can go (for medium and shoulder length hair, that is resting on your opposite shoulder).
3. Next **part** a small, diagonal section starting from the part in the front of your hair. **While holding the palm of your hand on the top of your head** (*very important* – to keep the loose hair from being pulled with the section you are wrapping), comb this section around the already wrapped hair that is resting at the base of your neck. Use a comb to gently rake the hair until it rests flat and smooth on top of the already wrapped hair.
4. **Repeat** step 3 until only a small section of hair is left (only the hair resting at the base of your neck should remain). After wrapping a couple of sections, gently smooth or **tighten the wrap** with your hands or a comb.
5. Take the remaining section and comb it around the already wrapped hair. Use your hands or a comb to **smooth and tighten the wrap**. You can smooth on a little oil like **Healthier Hair in a Bottle! Oil Spray**, if you like.
6. **Place bobby pins** in front and behind both ears to keep the wrap in place.
7. **Sit under hair dryer** until your hair is completely dry, the actual time depends on the length/thickness of your hair.
8. When dry, **gently unwrap** hair, using your fingers and/or a brush to smooth. You can also bump the ends if you like (see Styling section).
9. Style as desired, and spray hair lightly with **Isoplus Oil Sheen Hair Spray** or **Jheri Redding Volumizer Extra Shine** *Spray-On-Shine* for added sheen. *This is optional.*

If you want a straight style, with greater volume and incredible bounce and swing, and you have medium to long hair, try...

The Bubble Wrap Set

1. Find the largest size curlers your hair can hold. **Part sections**, and **set your hair** with them.
2. **Sit under the dryer** for about 20 minutes or longer, until your hair is at least ¾ dry.
3. **Remove the curlers** from your hair, and **gently comb** the curls out with your fingers.
4. Decide which direction you want your hair to hang or fall. Then **make a part** on the opposite side of your head in the front. Wrap in the opposite direction of the way you want it to hang or fall.
5. **Smooth hair** in the direction opposite to the way you want it to hang or fall. Use a wide-tooth comb to gently comb or smooth the hair from the side of the part towards the back of the neck. **Continue smoothing** until the hair lays flat. You can use your hands or a comb to gently smooth the hair. Make sure the length of your hair has been smoothed over as far as it can go (for medium and shoulder length hair, that is resting on your opposite shoulder).
6. Next part a small, diagonal section starting from the part in the front of your hair. **While holding the palm of your hand on the top of your head** *(very important – to keep the loose hair from being pulled with the section you are wrapping)*, comb this section around the already wrapped hair that is resting at the base of your neck. Use a comb to gently rake the hair until it rests flat and smooth on top of the already wrapped hair.
7. **Repeat** step 6 until only a small section of hair is left (only the hair resting at the base of your neck should remain). After wrapping a few sections, smooth/**tighten the wrap** with your hands or a comb.
8. **Comb** the remaining section around the already wrapped hair. Use your hands or a comb to **smooth and tighten the wrap**.
9. **Place bobby pins** in front and behind both ears to keep the wrap in place.
10. **Sit under hair dryer** until hair is completely dry, the actual time depends on the length/thickness of your hair.
11. When dry, **gently unwrap** hair, using your fingers and/or a brush to smooth.
12. **Style as desired**, and spray hair lightly with **Isoplus Oil Sheen Hair Spray** or **Jheri Redding Volumizer Extra Shine Spray-On-Shine** for added sheen. *This is optional.*

General Wet Setting Tips

- For smoother ends when using magnetic curlers or rods, you may want to use end papers.

- To shorten drying time, you might consider removing excess moisture from the hair before setting (e.g., wrap, plait, twist, etc.). To do this, part your hair down the middle or comb it from the center, where some is in the front and the rest is in the back or on the sides. For added heat protection and shine, you can spray on additional setting lotion or **Healthier Hair in a Bottle! Oil Spray.** Then either sit under a hair dryer, or use a blow dryer without the attachment to remove excess water from your hair. This could take as little as 10-15 minutes depending on how much drying time you wish to save. *Remember you are just removing excess moisture, not drying it. Then proceed with the steps for the set of your choice.*

- If your hair begins to dry as you are setting it, spray a small amount of your favorite setting lotion (e.g., Lottabody WRAP 'N TAP 'N Wrapping Lotion & Conditioner, Salon Finish *FOAM* Wrap & Style Lotion, etc.) as needed to re-wet it.

- Make sure your hair is completely dry before taking down your set and styling. If your hair is still damp, there is a greater chance for frizzing.

- For any of the wet sets you can oil your scalp with **Healthier Hair in a Bottle! Oil Spray** rubbing a little on the hair and ends before styling, if you like. Some stylists do, while others don't. I would, but you should let your hair and scalp be your guide.

BLOW DRYING

If you go to many salons blow drying is a very popular way of drying our hair, especially for shorter lengths. I think this is unfortunate as many women tend to blow dry and hot curl at home, so even at the salon our hair may not get a break from heat styling. The direct heat and pulling often associated with blow drying *can cause major damage to our hair*, especially if it is relaxed or color-treated. For this reason, *I only really recommend this method for sisters with natural hair.* Blow drying with a comb attachment can often help straighten natural hair enough for ladies and girls to wear a variety of styles, from pony-tails to curls. Also, many natural sisters blow dry their hair before straightening or pressing, with minimal damage, especially if they are careful. Of course, those of us with chemically-treated hair can use blow dryers *occasionally* to dry our hair straight and not suffer any significant damage, but **long-term, consistent use will lead to damage** (e.g., split-ends, breakage, etc.). So with the basic warnings out of the way, here are some blow drying steps:

1. Complete one of the shampooing and conditioning regimens in Chapter 3 (e.g., Week 1, Mid-Week/ Refresher, Swimmer's Hair Therapy, etc.).

2. Continue combing (use a very wide-tooth comb) through your favorite leave-in treatments and detangling your hair until it is relatively tangle-free and flat.

3. **NOTE:** *This step is optional, as some ladies may not wish to oil their scalp until after the hair is dry.* Part your hair in small sections, and oil your scalp with a very rich oil like **Healthier Hair in a Bottle! Oil Spray** (I used to use Wild Growth). After parting a section, I spray a few squirts onto my scalp, and rub it in. Before going to the next section, I rub a small amount of oil between my hands and rub it on the hair, especially the ends. When done, smooth any oil left on your hands on your edges and ends. *Make sure ends are well coated.*

4. Next, part the hair into 4 to 6 sections, and clip each section after combing (clipping is optional).

5. Using the blow dryer's comb attachments or your own wide-tooth comb, slowly comb through and blow dry each section. Direct the heat from the roots to the ends until hair is at least ¾ of the way dry. Keep in mind that your ends dry faster, so don't direct a lot of heat on them. Do not rush, and avoid excessive pulling.

General Blow Drying Tips:

- Choose a dryer with the lowest wattage needed to get the job done, *not the highest* – if given the choice between a 1250 watt dryer versus a 1650 watt dryer, *choose the 1250 watt one.* You may also want to consider trying the Ion dryers currently being advertised as safer, healthier blow drying alternatives.

- You may also want to try some of the thermal leave-in treatments on the market (e.g., Therma Silk, Paul Mitchell Seal and Shine, etc.)

- Gently towel dry hair and air dry or sit under a hooded dryer *before* blow drying to remove excess moisture. Comb through your hair and detangle like you normally would, just hold off on the actual blow drying. Let as much of the excess moisture dry from your hair as you can to limit the amount of time needed to blow dry. Even if you can wait as little as 15 minutes, there could be a great benefit in the long-term health of your hair. Women with chemically-treated hair should avoid using blow dryer attachments, *especially brushes.*

- Take your time as you comb through with blow dryer attachments, *especially if your hair is relaxed.* **Do not rush or handle your hair roughly**. Also, stay away from brush attachments. Because heat is being directly applied while you are combing, and *your hair is weakest while it is wet*, the potential for breakage is greater. If you are one of those ladies who does not use blow dryer attachments, try to keep the blow dryer at least 6 inches from your hair and scalp.

- Even if your hair is natural, slowly comb through the hair with a wide-tooth comb, spraying it with your favorite leave-in treatment or detangler (e.g., Infusium 23, Salon Finish Wrapping Lotion, Nu Expressions Wrapping Lotion, Healthier Hair in a Bottle! Moisturizing & Detangling Spray, etc.) as needed.

- Be sure to stop blow drying as soon as your hair feels dry – *overdrying your hair only causes damage.* Most styles will still work even if your hair is only 85 – 90% dry. See if yours will, if so, you will save your hair from possible damage by blow drying for shorter periods. You could let it air dry the rest of the way. This is a good thing, especially if you heat style more than a few times a week.

Chapter 5

DAILY HAIR CARE

Even though the Six-Week shampooing and conditioning regimen recommended in Chapter 3 will put you on the road to having beautiful, healthy, and even longer hair, you will not go far without a good daily hair care regimen. What you do *every* day – the products and treatments used, along with the styling and handling of your hair, actually determines how good your hair looks and how long it gets. To get the healthy, beautiful hair we seek, we all need to develop a daily hair care regimen designed just for us. In this chapter I share my daily hair care routine as well as tips and suggestions that will help you do just that. However, I must warn you that my regimen evolves as I learn more, and I am always on the lookout for new information, products and tips. So over the years I hope to continue sharing new information from my website even as I write about topics unrelated to hair care.

Tweaking the regimen I shared in the 1st edition of the book helped me to recover from some of the hair woes I encountered as I *foolishly* overprocessed my hair for a number of years and got lax about moisturizing. The tips and regimen shared in this chapter helped me get my hair to a *much* healthier state, enabling it to look decent on a daily basis. Since they worked so well, I made them the foundation of my new regimen. As with the Six-Week regimen in Chapter 3, feel free to use the information in this section as it is written or as an example to help you design the right regimen for you. Just in case you decide to follow it as written, you may need to purchase a few items.

Shopping List:

Select items from this list only as needed – at a minimum, get the first three items, and you will be off to a great start regardless of the regimen you decide to follow.

- The softest, smoothest boar bristle brush available (*if you can't find one, I sell the one I use from my website*)
- The widest tooth comb you can find (again, *if you can't find one, I sell the one I use from my website*)
- A satin scarf, cap or pillow cover or a thin plastic cap (shower or processing cap) – great for overnight ends treatments.

- **Healthier Hair in a Bottle! Oil Spray** – great for daily moisturizing and oiling the scalp. It is comparable to Wild Growth Hair Oil. It can be purchased from www.blackwomansguide.com. **Because this product contains Rosemary and Clary Sage, pregnant ladies should check with their ob/gyn before using, or use Wild Growth instead.**
- ***Healthier Hair in a Bottle! Moisturizing & Detangling Mist** – a great moisturizer and detangler that works wonderfully for daily combing of dry hair or for adding a moisture boost to natural or relaxed hair. It can be purchased from www.blackwomansguide.com.
- ***Healthier Hair in a Bottle! Ends Treatment** or Petroleum Jelly (e.g., Vaseline) – this is optional, but if you want *extra* ends protection or want your ends to have a nice polished finish this product is helpful.
- ***Ampro Pro-Style Marcel Wax** – optional, but wonderful if you do any type of heat styling. It gives ends a smooth, healthy-looking and polished finish, and curls last longer.
- ***A multi-vitamin supplement, such as GNC's Ultra NourishHair**
- ***Isoplus Oil Sheen Hair Spray** – a "nice-to-have" for extra shine.
- ***Jheri Redding Volumizer Extra Shine *Spray-On-Shine*** – again, a "nice-to-have" for extra shine and frizz protection.
- ***Fantasia IC Hair Polisher, Daily Hair Treatment** – another "nice-to-have" if you want a way to add shine without oil. It is a silicone-based product.
- ***Long Aid Curl Activator Gel w/ Aloe Vera** – great for smoothing down edges and "kitchen" control (you know, the hair at the back of your neck) if you wear buns or updos.

* Note: *Items marked with an asterisk are **optional** or nice-to-have items, only purchase them if you feel you need them.*

A Few Key Thoughts:

As you develop your own personal, daily hair care program there are a few overall important facts you should consider:

1. No *one* hair care product can guarantee perfect hair. So, don't believe ads for products that make these claims. Healthy, gorgeous hair is achieved through the use of a number of quality products, a *consistent* (not just whenever you feel like it) hair care regimen and having a *qualified* hair professional if chemical products are used.

2. All the hair care products in the world cannot replace good daily hair care, *no matter how good they are*. You cannot abuse your hair and expect even the best products to deliver on their claims. If you continue to use heat appliances every day, week after week, don't be surprised if the wonderful moisturizer that you are using, that claims to prevent split-ends and eliminate breakage, is not working. When you improve your overall hair care habits, you may start to experience some of the benefits claimed by the product manufacturers. However, you won't know until you adopt healthier hair care habits.

3. How you treat your body is just as important, *if not more*, as how you treat your hair. The best hair care regimen in the world will not be successful if you do not have a healthy diet that includes adequate water, protein and leafy-green vegetables (greens, broccoli, spinach, etc.). In fact, you should avoid diets that drastically restrict you from eating these foods. Also, for your health and hair's sake, drink at least eight glasses of water each day – soda and coffee do not count! If you don't like water, try it in a mug or tumbler with lots of ice (my kids and I love ice cold water), or add a slice of lemon or lime to it. No matter how you fix it, just drink it! Finally, a good multi-vitamin can help make up for any nutrient(s) that you may be lacking in your daily diet, so take one with a big glass of water and a meal (see more detailed information on vitamins in Chapter 9) – your hair will thank you!

4. Go easy on the chemicals, especially the relaxers and permanent coloring – a few wrong moves and your hair can get really "jacked up" fast, where you are left wondering what the heck happened. Both are best used *professionally* and as *rarely* as you can stand. Try to wait at least 8 weeks for relaxers if you can hold out that long, or as long as you can go without experiencing breakage. I have been getting touch-ups every 12-13 weeks now, as opposed to the 5-6 week schedule I had been on for 3 or 4 years. Foolishly, I mistook the *dryness* I saw and felt around week 4 or 5 of my relaxer as being unmanageable new growth, when it really was not. I have been amazed at how wetting my hair at least twice a week (shampooing or doing a cleansing rinse) and using **Healthier Hair in a Bottle! Oil Spray** a few times a week helped with that. *My hair was in need of additional moisture*, **not more chemicals**. I am sure that I am not the only one who has made this mistake. The tips in this chapter can help stretch the time between relaxers – they have for me. Waiting longer has made a big difference in the health of my hair, and I have also saved time and money. See chapter 7 for more on relaxing with care.

5. Leave the coloring or frosting of your hair to **professional** stylists. I remember when I was a teenager, my mother decided to color her own hair using a hair coloring product she found in the drug store. Next thing you know, she was covering a bald spot in the back of her head for months! Also, I remember, Kellie Shanygne Williams (Laura from TV's *Family Matters*) told a story in the March/April 1998 edition of *Sophisticate's Black Hair Styles and Care Guide* of a time where she tried to frost her hair using a drug store hair frosting kit. She had a bad experience too – her hair fell out at the root! According to the article this was one of the reasons she went with such a short hair cut. So for these and other reasons, I say if you can, leave the coloring or frosting to the professionals. Your hair is too important to take chances.

6. If you need to hide or cover gray hair, try a rinse or semi-permanent color before using a permanent color. For many women, permanent color can change the hair's texture for the worse. Before allowing me to graduate to semi-permanent coloring, my stylist used to have me sit under the dryer with a black coloring rinse to help it last longer. This worked until my stubborn gray hairs made me go semi-permanent. However, because my scalp has gotten more sensitive over the years, and the gray hairs start growing back within a week after getting semi-permanent color put in, I recently switched back to a rinse. My cousin recommended a product called Roux Fanci-Full Temporary Haircolor Rinse, which is sold in beauty supply stores. It is very gentle, comes in a number of different colors that can be shampooed out, can be applied at home, is not very messy, **and** contains a styling lotion. It has worked out to be the same difference for my hair, especially since I use a black touch-up wand to hook up the gray hair that grows around my edges. You probably can't even tell which pictures in this book or on my website show me with touched-up edges because it looks so natural when you brush it in. In case you are interested, the wands often look like oversized mascara tubes and can be bought pretty cheaply in most beauty supply stores. If rinses don't work for you, be sure to consult with a **professional** to apply semi-permanent and permanent color to minimize the risks and to help you decide which option or product(s) is best for you.

7. Speaking of coloring… I know some stylists say it is okay to color and relax at the same time, but I say *think again*. Based on some of my past experiences and some I have heard from other women, I don't think it is. I know it is convenient, and many coloring products claim that they can be used *safely* with relaxers, but their definition of "safely", and ours may be two different things. Theirs could just mean it won't make your hair fall out. However, it probably doesn't mean that your hair won't experience excessive dryness or shedding or that it won't become a little weaker or brittle. A few weeks after the procedure some of us might notice these types of conditions and think that we need more moisturizers or, worse, that it is time for a touch-up! Every woman's hair is different, and some of you might say I did it, and my hair was fine, and I believe that is the case for some of us, but a lot of us may not be that lucky. I wasn't, and if you have unexplained dryness, weak hair, excessive shedding or breakage, this could be an area to check.

With that said, let's go on to the tips and recommendations that should be the foundation for your daily hair care program:

HANDLING

A good policy for taking care of black hair (especially true for relaxed hair) is: "The less you handle it, the better." This specifically applies to combing and brushing. So in addition to saying be gentle when handling your hair (*it is more fragile than you think*), here are some tips that women with hair of all types can appreciate:

1. When combing your hair, use the widest tooth comb available. If you see a lot of hair in your comb after you use it or if you have a hard time combing through your hair, the teeth of your comb may be too close together. To further reduce breakage caused by combing, try detangling your hair with your fingers before combing. **If your hair is relaxed, you should avoid combing it all the way through more than 2 to 3 times a week.** Most days I just finger-comb my hair, and if your hair is well-conditioned, like it will be as you follow the *Six-Week Regimen*, you should be able to get away with this, especially for relaxed or fine hair.

2. When brushing your hair, use a soft boar-bristle brush. I mean the soft-bristled brushes that most black men use. You can also use some of the soft lint brushes (they resemble the men's brushes, but they are oval) – someone gave me one for Christmas, and I started using it on my son's hair, and now I use it. I never use the brushes usually marketed to women – natural or synthetic bristles. In fact, I never brush my hair all the way through. Have you ever noticed how much hair is in the brush after you thoroughly brush your hair? This is absolutely unnecessary! I used to watch television shows where white women brushed their hair every night before going to bed, and I wanted to do the same thing, thinking it would stimulate hair growth. For them, maybe – for us, no! Brushing's main purpose is to massage the scalp, distributing oils throughout the hair and to style hair (mainly by smoothing edges). For our sisters of other ethnic backgrounds, brushing may fulfill these purposes without major consequences. However, for black women, especially those of us with relaxed or color-treated hair, the consequence, over a long period of time, can be **major breakage**. So if you are trying to grow hair or maintain your current length, try replacing the brush with a gentle scalp massage (using your fingertips) a few times a week. Save the brush for times when you are wearing your hair pulled back, in an updo or when you are "gently" smoothing/flipping your ends for a specific style. During these times, gently brush the edges and smooth the hair where you need to. Otherwise, *don't use a brush*, especially on wet hair – trust me, you don't need it!

3. Detangle your hair *before* combing or brushing. You can make combing a lot easier by lightly misting your hair with **Healthier Hair in a Bottle! Moisturizing & Detangling Mist** (optional, even I only use it occasionally) and rubbing on a small amount of **Healthier Hair in a Bottle! Oil Spray**. Then separate hair into sections with your fingers. From there, start combing the ends first, and then gently work your way up the hair strand. Don't brush tangled strands of hair, instead mist the tangled section, gently straighten out the strands by pulling them together, and separate them with your fingers. Take your time because if you rush it becomes almost impossible to separate the tangle without cutting or breaking the strand, which causes you unnecessary breakage. This is very important when you do twist, plait or braid sets – I have experienced a few, and I have been getting better at undoing them, so I hope I can save you the trouble.

4. If you only comb through your hair a few times a week like me, you *could* see what looks like excessive shedding. Many sources say that the average person sheds between 75-100 strands of hair a day – this is

considered *normal* hair loss. Not saying that if you don't comb your hair for 3 days that you will lose close to 300 strands during the combout, but I am just preparing you that you may see more strands than you are used to seeing. By shedding I mean long or mature strands of hair coming out as you comb or detangle, some say with the white bulb (from your scalp) still on it. However, to be honest, I can only remember ever seeing one strand of hair with a bulb on it my entire adult life, and I almost freaked out, so I am not sure if that is an accurate way of judging, but you know what is *normal* for you. The normal rate of shedding has also been said to change seasonally and can also be affected by certain medications and conditions (e.g., oral contraceptives, anemia, etc.). Check with a dermatologist or your personal physician if you have questions or concerns about what you perceive to be excessive shedding and/or possible causes/solutions.

5. Have you seen advertisements for a product called the RevoStyler that claims to straighten, style and shine your hair in minutes? I have seen a couple of products similar to it that claim to have an *anti-tangle* system, where a brush rotates nearly 100 times a minute through your hair. They also claim that your hair will never tangle – even the thickest, curliest hair. They show a white model in the ads whose hair goes from a tangled mess to straight, silky-looking hair. I am sure for our sisters of other ethnic backgrounds it may work miracles, but I get scared every time I look at pictures of that product and think about it rotating 100 times a minute through the average black woman's hair, especially if our hair is relaxed! It sounds so wonderful in theory, but unless you are prepared to live with possible breakage, I would say pass. I must admit that I am curious, but just not brave enough to take a chance – not yet, anyway.

TREATMENTS

Your hair is truly a prized possession, and to see wonderful results, you must start treating it like the prize it is. Unfortunately, the focus today is slowly becoming for us to add to or cover up our hair to get the looks we want. Getting the "look" is not the most important thing – *taking care of our hair is*. This section will give some great tips to help you do just that, and hopefully Chapter 6 will help you get "the look" you are in search of. In the meantime:

1. Moisturize your hair and ends *everyday*. Most mornings I massage my scalp with a little **Healthier Hair in a Bottle! Oil Spray** (you can use this or a similar oil). Then depending on how my hair feels, I might lightly spray sections of my hair with **Healthier Hair in a Bottle! Moisturizing & Detangling Mist** (optional) as I detangle it. Either way, I smooth the oil spray onto 4-8 sections of my hair from root to end (I have also used extra virgin olive oil and various products by Profectiv, which all work relatively well for moisturizing too).

   If I plan to curl my hair, I gently comb and section it before using the Caruso Steam Hair Setter (see Chapter 6 for details). Most times I put a little wax on the ends of each section before curling for hold and a nice polished look. After removing the curlers, I *sometimes* spray my hair with **Isoplus Oil Sheen Hair Spray** if it is humid or rainy or I need extra shine. I might also spray on the **Jheri Redding Volumizer** after styling. *Both of these sprays are optional, and I don't use them on a regular basis.*

   To seal in moisture for my ends and to give them added protection, after styling, I *might* also smooth on a small amount of **Healthier Hair in a Bottle! Ends Treatment** (I have also used **Vaseline**) onto my ends (not all of them, just the ones that can be easily isolated in my style). Talk about hair looking good! Try it some time and be impressed.

2. Moisturize every day *even if you don't curl your hair*. To be honest, most days I don't curl my hair, I just try to recycle styles (finger-comb and fluff the curls from yesterday or the day before that). On those days, I *might* mist my hair, detangle and rub on some oil spray. At a minimum, I would use a light oil product for a scalp massage and to smooth on the hair itself. If needed, I *might* put an ends treatment or **Vaseline** on the ends, and call it a day. It just depends on how the hair is *looking* and *feeling* – this is how you decide, which if any, of these products should be used.

   Other days, if I am wearing my hair in an updo or bun (very rarely, unless it is very cold) and it is close to a shampoo, I *might* put curl activator on my edges and ends after using the **Healthier Hair in a Bottle!** products. This allows you to create some cute slick styles, especially if you are trying to make it until the next shampoo or until the next touch-up. After a few months of experimenting with these or similar products, what you see in the mirror in the morning will help you determine which products you need for the day. However, as a rule, you should *use at least one moisturizing product daily*, especially if heat styling tools are used.

3. Don't neglect your scalp. You can't have healthy hair without a *healthy* scalp. For relaxed hair, especially, the scalp should be oiled once or twice a week depending on how dry it is. I do not recommend "grease" or heavy pomades because they don't allow the scalp to breathe, which could slow down hair growth and cause the scalp to flake and itch. These types of products can also weigh the hair down, making it too heavy, causing curls to fall faster. I recommend oiling the scalp with **Healthier Hair in a Bottle! Oil Spray** or **Wild Growth Hair Oil** (your choice), but I now use **Healthier Hair in a Bottle! Oil Spray** at least twice a week – once after shampooing and again mid-week. Depending on the condition of your hair and scalp, you can do more or less.

   I also massage a little oil spray into my scalp after I get a touch-up (*after* the hair is styled). Many stylists do not oil the scalp after relaxers are put in, but for most women the scalp and hair will need a light oiling. So after each touch-up, massage a little **Healthier Hair in a Bottle! Oil Spray** into the scalp and on the hair itself. This oil helps to improve the condition of your scalp and the overall feel of your hair, especially for new growth. It can be used as often as needed. You can also try virgin olive oil or other rich oils like coconut, avocado or apricot. However, you should avoid products that contain mineral oil as it is **not** a natural oil. It *can* (not saying that it always does) clog hair follicles, slow down hair growth and interfere with your scalp's natural function.

   I used to oil my scalp with **Wild Growth Hair Oil**, but because I used it so much with the Pony-Tail method, the smell started to really bother me. I do have to give it up to the makers of **Wild Growth** because their product was the first one I was able to use to air dry my hair straight. However, one night I realized as I was talking to someone at my sons' school that not only was the oil running down my face, but I was also noticeably stinky from it! My husband had already been complaining about the smell, and one night in bed, he even had the nerve to ask if one of the boys had an "accident" in our bed. For a short while he used it on his hair and our boys', but he stopped because he thought it smelled like urine. So needless to say I was embarrassed and immediately started looking for a replacement, which is how I wound up developing **Healthier Hair in a Bottle! Oil Spray.**

4. Let your scalp breath! Do not wear a wig more than two to three times a week and no more than eight to ten hours a day. After each wear, massage your scalp with a little **Healthier Hair in a Bottle! Oil Spray**, putting a light coating on the ends of your hair. Also, adding a little moisture to your hair with **Healthier Hair in a Bottle! Moisturizing & Detangling Mist** beforehand may be beneficial as well.

5. Don't forget to treat your hairline (edges), which is subjected to a lot of stress when hair is pulled back or when headbands are used. Whenever the scalp is oiled or a night-time treatment is used, remember to massage this area. Avoid pulling hair back or using a headband in the same style for more than three to four times a week – this will help prevent breakage or patches along the hairline. As a healthier alternative to headbands, I have found *Ouchless* headbands by Goody (an elastic circle covered by fabric) to be a good choice, and they work as pony-tail holders too. I have also thought of cutting a thin strip of satin to make a ribbon that can be wrapped around my head. The goal is to come up with ways to change your hairstyle without damaging your hair. Wearing a variety of styles can definitely help you avoid hairline troubles.

6. If you have had problems with thinning, the **Healthier Hair in a Bottle! Oil Spray** can also be used for scalp massages in areas where there is thinning or bald spots. Last year when I noticed some thinning around my front edges, I started massaging the area with this oil in the morning and night, and after a few weeks, I noticed that *baby* hair started growing in. This was amazing to me since I was 37 at the time! Since then my hair has continued to fill in where I had problems, but finding the source of thinning problems (e.g., overprocessing, wearing the hair pulled too tightly, etc.) is the best way to keep you from dealing with more serious hair complaints in the future (e.g., bald spots, etc.). For more serious problems, especially ones you can't pinpoint a cause, be sure to visit a dermatologist or your physician for advice.

7. Try this treatment at least once a week: Before taking a shower rub on a little **Healthier Hair in a Bottle! Oil Spray** or a similar oil (I used to use Fantasia IC P.M. Night-Time Oil Treatment before I realized that it contains mineral oil), and put on a shower cap. The steam from the shower will give your hair a mini hot-oil treatment before you style it.

8. Before spending time at the beach, you might want to rub a small amount of **Fantasia IC Hair Polisher, Daily Hair Treatment** or **Healthier Hair in a Bottle! Oil Spray** on your hair for heat protection (both contain sunscreen and other moisturizers). However, if you will spend a great deal of time in the sun or will be swimming, you could also use a leave-in conditioner such as **Infusium 23** or **All Ways 911 Emergency Hair & Scalp Treatment**. *If you swim without a cap, make sure you shampoo and condition afterwards.*

ENDS MAINTENANCE

1. I used to recommend trimming your ends every four to eight weeks, almost as if to imply that all women's hair, growth rate and regimens are the same. I have since realized that *they are not*. I now recommend that split, weakened or damaged ends should be cut whenever they are spotted. This could be every four weeks, six weeks or even twelve weeks or longer, it just depends on how well you treat your hair and protect your ends. Your stylist should check for them at every visit (e.g., when getting a touch-up, color, etc.), or you should if you have been trained to do so. However, if your ends are not split, damaged or raggedy-looking, they do not necessarily have to be trimmed, *unless you want them to be.*

    Many stylists recommend having trims every 6-8 weeks to ensure optimal hair growth, but women who have healthy hair habits are beginning to realize that trimming the ends **does not** affect the *growth* of our hair. I did not really begin to think about and research this until after I wrote my first book. I started to notice that no matter how well I took care of my hair, almost any stylist I went to seemed ready and willing to trim off just as much as when I used to abuse my hair. It seemed almost like an unspoken ritual – trim if the ends seem dry, if there is any frizz, or if the ends are uneven. I noticed this even with the stylist I go to regularly so I decided to visit a few other stylists (unfortunately, without talking to my stylist first) to see if their approach would be different. This only made matters worse because the new stylist whacked off at least 2 inches (I think she mistook the frizz from a twist set for damaged ends. I tell you, one visit to the wrong stylist can undo months of hard work.

This experience left me desperate, so I turned to the Internet where I read a comment made by Cathy Howse (another hair care author) regarding **not** trimming ends. As I read some of her comments, I decided to put my own ends to the test to see how long I could go without trimming and **not** getting split ends. I went back to my old stylist and fessed up about my concerns with my hair staying practically the same length as she trimmed it *even though she would always say my ends looked good*. She and I worked out a plan where she would not trim my ends until she saw split-ends. As a result, I did not have a trim for over 5 months. The results: my hair finally grew past my bra strap, but because I was not practicing good ends maintenance and had backslidden on some of my daily hair treatments, *my ends*, although not split, *were raggedy and uneven looking*, **but the hair was growing**. So at my next hair appointment, I had about an inch taken off to even up my ends, giving my hair a healthier, more even look, and I vowed to follow the tips I am outlining in this section on ends maintenance more carefully!

If taken care of properly, our ends may only need to be trimmed a few times a year. I have heard of many women who are doing this, and their hair is reaching incredible lengths. So all of this to say that *when* you trim should be up to **you** and your stylist. If you are trying to grow your hair longer, be sure to ask questions about the condition of your ends and the necessity or purpose of a trim. Also, let your stylist know your goals regarding hair growth. I say this because constant trimming, when the ends are healthy, can keep your hair at the same length for years. For women who like a blunt cut or all of the ends to be even, this is fine, but for those trying to grow their hair longer it is not. If a sister does not realize what is going on, this trimming of healthy ends could give the impression that our hair does not grow like everyone else', and *that is not true – our hair does grow just like everyone else's! If it didn't, none of us would ever need a touch-up.* All of that to say, when trims are necessary, be sure to have them because this simple task can help keep our ends strong and healthy.

2. At least 3 or 4 nights a week separate hair into sections, and spray **Healthier Hair in a Bottle! Oil Spray** into hands and massage a little into the scalp and smooth it from roots to ends, paying special attention to the ends. Then put a little **Healthier Hair in a Bottle! Ends Treatment** or **Vaseline** on the bottom two inches of the hair, and put on a thin plastic cap (a shower cap like people with Jheri curls used to use) or a satin scarf/cap/bonnet (if you prefer that) before going to bed. This will give your ends a very nice moisturizing treatment that can counteract exposure to the elements (e.g., sun, wind and cold). I do this treatment a lot during the winter because I don't like to wear *protective* styles (i.e., styles where your ends are tucked in) a lot. I tried them for a few days, but I realized that I don't like to wear my hair in the same style for long periods of time, and I have heard women complain of thinning caused from pulling the hair back in buns too frequently. So if you wear your hair down/loose a lot, this treatment can help to reduce breakage and split-ends. However, you should still monitor your ends for dryness throughout the week, and increase/reduce this treatment as needed. Dry, brittle ends break and split – so this treatment is very important. Also, if you are trying to sustain major hair growth, your ends will require a lot of protection, and this treatment is a good way to do this.

3. If you wear your hair down/loose in a windy, hot or dry environment, you may want to give your ends a moisture boost by spraying a little **Healthier Hair in a Bottle! Moisturizing & Detangling Mist** onto your hair and ends a few times during the day as needed. I did this a few times a day while I vacationed at the beach to keep my hair hydrated. Afterwards, I would sometimes rub a little **Healthier Hair in a Bottle! Oil Spray** onto the ends for extra protection. For those who are wondering, relaxed hair remains straight after this treatment as long as you just mist your hair, not soak it. If there is any frizz on the ends, I smooth it down with the **Healthier Hair in a Bottle! Ends Treatment** or **Vaseline**, whichever I have handy. This treatment

is also good for those who wear braids. However, no one should feel they have to use all three products to experience benefits – *use only the products you feel your hair needs at the time.*

4. Protect your hair while you sleep, whether your hair is natural or relaxed, whether you wear weaves, extensions or braids, pillow cases and sheets can dry out hair, *especially your ends.* Even when satin pillowcases and sheets are used, your hair is still subjected to the friction caused by the weight of your head against the fabric. Because of this, I suggest you wear a satin cap, scarf or a thin shower cap to bed after putting on an oil like **Healthier Hair in a Bottle! Oil Spray** or olive oil and a small amount of **Healthier Hair in a Bottle! Ends Treatment** or **Vaseline** on the ends at least 3 or 4 times a week. I am talking about the real thin caps like you find in hotels that have very loose elastic. I have found those to put less stress on the hairline, an area where I have had problems. I let the elastic rest a few inches above the front edges, closer to the middle of my head, which should prevent any dampness that some ladies could experience (it depends on how much sweating you do – I sweat a lot, but my hair is never damp in the morning). I know this is reminiscent of the days when people wore Jheri curls, but, as it did then, this process seals in moisture, acting like an overnight mini-hot oil treatment, especially when you use oils that your hair can easily absorb (e.g., jojoba, apricot, olive, etc.).

    To be honest, I even put on a cap or use my satin pillow cover when I take a nap or lie in the bed to read. Protecting your hair in this way not only minimizes breakage, but it also helps you cut down on the use of heat styling tools by preserving hairstyles. As a special note for vain women who may not want to be seen wearing a cap or scarf at night, do what I do: After my husband and I turn off the light before bed, I put on my thin plastic cap (I keep it under the pillow). Other nights I put it on with him looking, and **yes he makes jokes**, but he is not complaining because my hair looks better at 37 (although it is a lot grayer) than it did when I was 19 (when he first met me). Protect your hair at night consistently, and you should see a noticeable improvement in your hair too! Combined with trimming hair as needed, minimal combing/brushing, and limited heat styling, this treatment is a great way to minimize split-ends and breakage.

5. If you choose not to use a satin pillow cover and don't wear a cap to bed, you can still provide some protection to your ends and hairstyle by pulling or securing the curls up high on your head so they are not touching the pillow.

6. In addition to all of the treatments and tips above, be sure to monitor your ends for dryness **every** day. If they need more moisture, be sure to moisturize as often as needed. However, if moisturizing does not work, this could be a good sign that your hair is in need of a shampoo or cleansing rinse, especially if you use styling products like mousse, gel, or spritzes or if you sweat a lot. The look and feel of our ends can often tell us where we are going wrong in our regimen (e.g., not moisturizing enough, blow drying and hot curling too often, etc.). Always be on the look out for clues, and change your habits accordingly.

7. If an outfit, jacket, coat, necklace or car/furniture upholstery catches on your hair or constantly snags it, make sure you pull your hair up or out of the way of the offending item as soon as possible. Unnecessary breakage is often experienced from items that seem harmless. Sometimes, I notice if I am wearing my hair straight, and depending on the car I am riding in, seat upholstery or a shoulder strap can catch or pull strands of my hair. To avoid this, I pull it around to the front, or I might twist it into a bun or pin it up until I am out of the car. Another seemingly harmless thing is a broken or split nail that needs to be filed. Jagged nails can do quite a bit of damage as you are detangling, finger-combing or styling your hair, so make sure you file them as needed before handling your hair. Another example is a cute necklace I have that gets so tangled in my hair when I wear it down that I have to spend a good amount of time just trying to get loose. Even then, I still usually wind up breaking at least 2 or 3 strands. As a result, I wear my hair up whenever I wear this necklace. I know a few broken strands may not seem like much, but over time, if it happens enough, you will see a

difference in how even and thick your ends look when your hair is straight. Not only can ends look uneven, but stylists may be tempted to trim more to even the ends up. However, a few simple workarounds can make a big difference in how healthy your ends look and how much length you retain.

STYLING

Because most hair damage occurs during day-to-day styling, here are some styling tips that might help protect your hair:

1. **Avoid heat styling tools like the plague!** This includes curling irons, flat irons and electric curlers. Do not use these appliances more than two or three times a week – they are very damaging to your hair. As often as possible replace these appliances with the Caruso Steam Hair Setter, or wrap sets for straight hair styles, and overnight sets like a twist or plait/braid set (see Chapters 4 or 6 for alternatives and "how-to" information) for curlier styles. You could also check out some of the soft curlers found in local beauty supply, discount and drug stores – examples include products like *Solar Rollers for Spirals, Hair Twirlers* and *Pillow Soft Rollers* to create spiral curls or a soft curly set. Even if you don't want to completely give up your curling iron and flat iron, cutting down to just once or twice a week can still improve the overall health of your hair. Once you get used to using products like the Caruso Hair Setter, you will also see a big time savings – it used to take me over 30 minutes to curl my entire head, but now I can have curls that last for days in less than 15 minutes. I will show styles and give instructions on using this product in Chapter 6.

2. If you continue to use curling irons, do **not** look for the hottest one you can find. I know some of the ones sold in beauty supply stores claim to get hotter than regular irons. Try to avoid those – they burn faster and can cause more damage to your hair, scalp and skin (*I had a roommate in college who had burn marks near her hairline on a regular basis*). To be safe, regardless of the curling iron, be sure to test it first by touching it with a paper or cloth towel *before* it touches your hair. If it burns the towel it is too hot for your hair. ***Let it cool first, and then curl with care.***

3. Do not use hot curling appliances (i.e., electric curlers, curling irons, flat irons or crimping irons) on dirty or excessively dry hair (hair that has not been washed for one or more weeks). There are a number of reasons why I say this: 1) Your hair is already in a vulnerable state when it is dirty because it may be drier than normal, and heat styling will only dry it out more, possibly causing breakage or damage; and 2) The buildup of oils and dirt on hair that has not been washed usually makes it difficult to curl, requiring you to use more heat than normal, which, again, subjects your hair to possible breakage or damage. Why take a chance? Give your hair a break, and hydrate it with a good shampoo (could also be a cleansing rinse) before subjecting it to heat styling – your hair *will* definitely appreciate it. However, if it is not dirty, maybe it is just feels dry, try misting it with **Healthier Hair in a Bottle! Moisturizing & Detangling Mist** about ten minutes before curling to give it some added moisture, and then smooth on a little **Healthier Hair in a Bottle! Oil Spray** mainly to the ends. A moisture mist dries very quickly so your hair should actually be dry by the time you start curling – to be safe start curling the area you sprayed first. I think one of the reasons other groups of women don't often experience the same types of damage we do from heat styling is because they are forced to shampoo (hydrate the hair) their hair more often. So if you are going to continue heat styling, make sure your hair is prepared to withstand the heat. Even if you don't use either of the products mentioned above, a hair wax such as **Ampro Pro-Style Marcel Wax** can protect your ends and give you a very smooth finish and longer lasting curls.

4. If you do use curling appliances always protect your hair first with a good moisturizer at least 10 minutes before. I noticed the last time I got a touch-up that my stylist put **Ampro Pro Styl Marcel Wax** (a scarlet red product in a clear jar) on my ends to protect them from the heat of the flat iron. It can be used with curling irons as well. It also seems to work well to smooth edges, and the label claims that it helps prevent edges from reverting back because of moisture.

5. If you decide to follow the same steps in #3, while the hair is still damp from the mist and oil sprays, you could also put in soft curlers, rollers, plaits or twists instead. While it is drying, do the things you normally do to get ready (e.g., take a shower, put on makeup, etc.). By the time it dries (10-15 minutes), you could have a pretty decent set of curls, twists or spirals, depending on how you chose to set it. I did this while on vacation at the beach using twists, and I was surprised at how quickly my hair set. I think it is worth a try as a healthier and quicker styling alternative. I am thinking that as I do one of these quick sets, it would also be a great *time to test out a new product*, **Aubrey Organics Natural Body Highlighter Mousse**. I bought *Soft Black* to cover my gray in between shampoos. It is an all natural product that can be used on dry or damp hair, and it claims to condition, add luster and give long-lasting body. So I am going to give it a try soon!

6. If you wear curlers/rollers to bed at night, make sure they are soft and are not so tight that they put stress on your scalp. Also, make sure that you don't wear them to bed more than a few times a week. Just like tight braids or extensions, they can put unnecessary stress on your scalp. I saw some satin curlers made by *Hype Hair* that seem like they might be safe enough for overnight use. Just be careful, and don't ignore any warning signs (e.g., thinning, breakage, etc.).

7. Do not use sprays, mousses or gels that contain alcohol – they can dry hair out, and cause breakage. When selecting sprays, choose silicone-based products for maximum shine. Although I have not used mousse for a number of years, as I mentioned earlier, I am getting ready to try **Aubrey Organics Natural Body Highlighter Mousse** to see how well it works (*I will give feedback on my website after I have a conclusive opinion*). It does not contain alcohol, and it is supposed to highlight your natural hair coloring, *and their other products are good*, so it might be a good one to try. Regardless of what you try, do not use any hair product that makes your hair hard, brittle or sticky. Any product that does this should be removed from your hair care regimen because it will eventually cause breakage. If your hair is well conditioned, it should lay flat for most pulled back styles without pomades or gels. It should also maintain its style without large amounts of hair spray. However, if your edges need more help to lay flat, try some of the popular curl activator products (Long Aid and S-Curl are brands you could try) – read labels and select the best one for you. You can also use a little **Vaseline** alone or mixed with water. Once applied, gently smooth the edges with a very soft brush. Surprisingly, **Vaseline** is effective and leaves your hair soft and easy to restyle, unlike most gels.

8. Instead of holding sprays, try to use products like **Isoplus Oil Sheen** or **Volumizer Extra Shine Spray-On-Shine** by Jheri Redding for sheen. Even though there are holding sprays without alcohol, they can still make the hair hard. For that reason, I never use holding sprays, only oil sheen. This was not always the case – in high school I was the queen of the "tuck comb", and then in college, of holding spray and bobby pins because my hair was always "all over my head". However, once I started setting my hair with the Caruso Steam Hair Setter, I noticed that my normally fly-away, unruly hair began to stay in place without holding sprays. Don't get me wrong, the curls still blow in the wind, but they either fall back into place on their own, or I can easily finger-comb them back into place. Try the Caruso Steam Hair Setter along with tips in this chapter and Chapter 6, and see if you can live without holding sprays. If you can, you may see a big difference in the condition of your hair and ends.

9. After styling, you can protect exposed ends (you don't have to mess up your style, just the ends that are hanging out) or smooth down frizz by rubbing a small amount of **Healthier Hair in a Bottle! Ends**

Treatment or **Vaseline** on the ends. This is a good finishing step. Not only are your ends protected, but your finished style looks more polished. This step is essential during the winter if you don't wear protective styles.

10. Even if you choose not to style your hair on a regular basis and either let it hang or put it in a pony-tail, try to at least bump the ends so they are not as isolated and exposed to possible damage. Think of a rope, which is a lot stronger than the individual strands it is made of. Well, curled ends are grouped together kind of like a rope, *not in isolated strands*, which makes them a little stronger, less likely to break.

11. If it is very cold or windy outside, try to wear hairstyles that protect your ends, like updos or buns. For those who are not experts at creating updos (myself included), I have found a quick way to protect my ends and create looks that can be professional, elegant or casual. Start by moisturizing your hair. Then get a bow that is close to your hair color, and finger-comb your hair, pulling it back with the bow. Separate the pony-tail into sections (at least two, and no more than six) and loosely wrap each section around the base of the bow. This is not an exact science so you can have all sections going in one direction, or some of the sections going in different directions. You can also wrap the sections loosely or firmly. Also try putting the bow at different places on your head – high, near the front, at the center of your head or at the nape of your neck. Once you practice this a few times, the finished product will look as though you have more hair than you do and that you spent more time creating this look than you did.

12. Avoid pulling hair back tightly or using a headband (this used to be my biggest weakness, *headbands make styling so much easier*) in the same style more than 3 to 4 times a week. Wearing a variety of styles helps prevent breakage or patches along the hairline. This is especially important for little girls, who all too many times have their hair pulled into very tight pony-tails which can cause traction alopecia. Sometimes I hear our young girls talking about how their pony-tails or braids are so tight that they don't want you to touch them – because they hurt. We are the only group I know that subjects our children to such painful styles. *I believe our girls can still be cute without being in pain.* Many times the girls I see with the tightest pony-tails usually have short hair that is thin or patchy around the edges. The sad irony is that many of the parents wonder why their child's hair won't grow! I know old habits die hard, but to avoid long-term scalp damage, I say loosen up those pony-tails – for all ages!

13. When pulling hair back, do not use rubber bands or any other hair accessories that might cause hair to break. Instead, use coated bands, fabric bows or clips. Also, try to use loose fitting headbands – this is important for women with large, round heads (*like me*). I have started using the *Ouchless* Headband by Goody. You can find them at Wal-Mart or wherever Goody products or sold (e.g., grocery store, drugstore, etc.). Try to avoid wide, tight head bands – the thinner/skinnier they are, the better. Finally, do not use the circular headbands that have teeth that fit on top of your hair – the teeth on these headbands or hair ornaments tend to pull the hair pretty tightly and can get tangled in the process.

14. When using bobby pins to secure your hair in updos or buns, do not use pins with the plastic tips removed. Also to help minimize unnecessary breakage, try stretching the pins so that the tips don't touch. Better still, try using hair pins, which are already stretched apart.

15. Treat your hair to a "day-time rejuvenator" by applying a small amount of **Fantasia IC Hair Polisher, Daily Hair Treatment** to your already-styled hair and ends. This can give life and shine to your existing hairstyle (as an example if you are re-styling before going out), while providing extra protection to your ends.

16. To preserve styles overnight, push or loosely secure curls on top of the head so that the weight of your head does not crush them while you are sleeping. For extra protection cover your hair with a satin cap/scarf or a thin plastic cap (I just started doing the plastic cap thing over the past year). In the morning, lightly

moisturize and massage the scalp. Then finger-comb your hair into the style of your choice. To preserve your straight styles, before putting on the cap of your choice (e.g., satin or plastic), many women wrap their hair (I give very basic instructions for a variation of it in Chapters 4 and 6). This can work for your hair as well as it does for weaves and extensions. It also helps minimize tangling.

17. **Do not use weaves or braids that require glue or that pull your hair very tightly.** If someone is braiding your hair too tightly, tell them immediately. Also, do not add lengthy or heavy extensions/braids onto weak, thinning or damaged hair.

18. If you wear a weave, extensions or braids, shampoo, deep condition and moisturize your hair like you normally would or according to the instructions of your stylist. Do not leave the braids or extensions in longer than 6-8 weeks. Also, if extensions or braids cannot be washed, do not wear them for more than two weeks.

19. If possible, use human hair for your weave styling. Human hair not only looks more natural, but it also gives more flexibility in styling, lasts longer and allows you to use heat styling tools on it (e.g., curling irons, electric curlers, etc.).

20. Do not wear weaves, wigs and extensions every day for long periods, only wear them occasionally. I know advertisements for *instant, wonder* or *quick* weaves and large wig selections are very tempting as we try to get the latest styles and maintain them faster and easier. However, I really believe these items of convenience are turning into a trap for too many of us. I am so annoyed by the numerous and constant ads in popular black magazines for weaves, wigs or extensions – *you don't see this as much in magazines targeting white audiences of similar age groups*. There are just as many of these ads in our magazines as there are for actual hair care products. I feel the message being sent to us and to our young girls is that it is too hard to grow and maintain our own hair, so we should just give up and rely on store-bought hair to solve our hair care woes. I disagree with this way of thinking because **we can take care of our own hair, with less effort than we think, and it can look good!**

Our hair can be healthy and stylish, and yes, it can grow long if we practice good hair care habits! I want to see more of us sporting our own hair regardless of the length or texture – it doesn't have to be long, just healthy. As an example, I saw a beautiful actress in a movie called "Lift" on BET recently, I believe her name was Kerry Washington. I remember being really impressed with her acting ability, but also by the fact that she was sporting her own hair. I can't remember seeing a lot of *our* actresses wearing just their own hair, but it was very refreshing to see, especially since her hair was more of a short to medium length in the movie. She reminded me of Nia Long, who was also really cute in the movie "Big Momma's House" wearing what seemed to be *just* her hair. **I think one of the healthiest things we can do for our hair is to find a style that looks good using just *our own* hair and maintain it**, hopefully with the help of this book and a good stylist this will be easier. This whole added hair craze is taking our focus off of taking care of our own hair, which means that our hair is often neglected as we try to keep the added on hair looking good – this is just too big of a distraction for most women. However, it does not often become obvious (e.g., receding hairlines, damaged ends, etc.) until after the *added* hair is removed. I don't mean to "preach", but this is such a troubling trend. Occasional use is fine, but if used long-term, we are begging for trouble. If this tip/rant only helps one person to realize that taking care of our hair is not a hopeless cause, then I will say, "mission accomplished."

21. Before getting your hair braided, oil your scalp with **Healthier Hair in a Bottle! Oil Spray**, and mist sections of hair with **Healthier Hair in a Bottle! Moisturizing & Detangling Spray** for easier detangling and braiding (optional). Rub some of the oil spray (or a similar oil) on individual sections of hair as needed. Do

not use gels or heavy greases/pomades though because they can leave a residue on braids. After shampooing and blow/air drying braids you can do pretty much the same thing – lightly oil your scalp, massage and moisturize the hair. To keep your braids shiny on a daily basis, you can also rub **Healthier Hair in a Bottle! Oil Spray** or some other oil of your choice (e.g., olive oil, etc.) into individual braids as needed.

22. Don't neglect braids, weaves or extensions. Make sure you keep them *and* your hair moisturized according to the instructions of your stylist. In cases where you did not get instructions, or you added the hair yourself, you can use most of the products I recommend for your hair on the "added" hair. However, to be safe you could look on the purchased hair's label or product labels for clues as to whether certain products are suitable for the type of hair you have added (e.g., synthetic extensions, etc.). One of the products I used to use and recommended that specifically mentioned braids/weaves/extensions is the **Fantasia IC P.M. Night-Time Oil Treatment**, which says that it gives extensions, braids and weaves a smoother look and feel. However, because this product contains mineral oil, I have stopped using and recommending it. If you decide to try it, you could use it as you would on your normal hair. However, I think that the **Healthier Hair in a Bottle! Oil Spray** will work just as well, if not better for moisturizing your scalp, hair and added hair, but you can be the judge. Regardless, as a rule, take care of "added" hair like you do your own; otherwise, you may damage your own!

23. If you are using the braid/extension tips for young or teenage girls make sure that you are not damaging their hair and scalp with heavy extensions, braids and/or ornaments (e.g., heavy beads, tight rubber bands, etc.). It is amazing that a child, or even an adult, with hair that is maybe four inches long or shorter would have heavy extensions that are three or four times that length. Doing this can cause long-term scalp damage and eventually slow down hair growth. To reduce your risk, consult with a trained extension/braid expert on the best lengths for your hair, scalp and age. Also, at the first sign of trouble, don't hesitate to visit a dermatologist. What you do today may seem like a harmless style, but down the road, it could mean major hair/scalp problems for you or your child, so I say you can't be too careful.

24. Although I have never worn a wig before, I have seen family members suffer from hair ailments related to overusing them. Just looking at the inside of a wig cap, it seems like it could be very drying to hair, especially if worn directly on top of the hair or even with a stocking cap. As a result, I was wondering for those who *occasionally* wear wigs, how would it work if you wore the thin shower cap I mentioned as an ends moisturizing treatment under the wig? The only reason I suggest this is because last winter I often wore a black beret to protect my hair from the bitter cold weather we experienced. Because it was made of wool, I moisturized my hair like normal and put on a thin shower cap underneath. No one could tell the difference. Of course, I would have been embarrassed if someone pulled it off, but it kept my hair and ends from being exposed to the wool. When I went somewhere and I wanted to take it off and let my hair down, I would excuse myself so I could do it in private. I don't know how well it will work, but it may be worth a try to keep your hair protected while wearing wigs. I think it is an important concern because long-term wig wearers often experience problems related to the friction placed on their natural hair while wearing wigs (e.g., thinning, pattern baldness, breakage, dryness, etc.). You can't be too careful. I would love to hear if this works for someone out there.

25. When teasing hair, use a very wide toothed comb. For hairstyles where you have teased your hair, take plenty of time to gently comb out the style. Teased hair is in a very fragile state, and it can be easily broken. The same goes for hair that has been gelled or sprayed with holding spray. Try to get at least two to three days out of styles like these, meaning try not to comb them out, just re-wear them for a few days by either finger-combing or by gently combing the ends. I used to "recycle" hairstyles a lot by using headbands, but now I might pull my hair back or wear all or parts of it in an up-do. By learning to recycle hairstyles, you can

significantly reduce the time you spend heat styling or combing – hopefully, to no more than once or twice a week.

26. If you do tease your hair, you might want to periodically replace teasing with separating curls into multiple, thinner strands and fluffing them with your fingers. This can create the same kind of fullness and volume that teasing can, without the tangles or the risk of breakage/damage. Separating curls also allows you to create different looks with your normal sets, without teasing or combing.

27. In addition to the tips above, for medium to long lengths (straight or curly styles), you can also create major volume and fullness by flipping your head forward (allowing your hair to hang upside down) and finger-combing your hair to the front. You can mist it first with **Healthier Hair in a Bottle! Moisturizing & Detangling Spray** and/or rub on some **Healthier Hair in a Bottle! Oil Spray** if it looks or feels dry. Gently start from the nape of your neck and work your fingers through to the front of your head. Then flip your head back, and finger-comb the front into the style of your choice. You can add a headband and slightly push the hair forward or twist the hair in the front, with the back full and bouncy, creating some really cute looks. I call this the "white girl effect" because I saw one of my white college roommates do this to "fluff" her hair. I wondered what it would do to my hair, so I tried it (in private of course!). I was surprised to find that it actually added body and swing to many of my hair styles. It also helped me to "fix" a number of styles that did not turn out right. You can laugh if you want to, but I suggest you try it a couple of times (in private of course) – you don't have to have long hair either. I think you may be pleasantly surprised.

   Note: This trick does not work well if you are in desperate need of a touch-up. Instead of having a fluffy style, full of body, you could end up looking like Don King! So your roots need to be relatively straight to do this.

28. To prevent your hair from frizzing during workouts, pull your hair firmly back, away from your face, with your roots lying flat *before you start exercising*. I usually smooth on a little **Healthier Hair in a Bottle! Oil Spray** (I am sure you could also try other oils) to help prevent my hair from absorbing as much sweat. Be sure to keep your ends dry by wrapping them or pinning them up on your head. Leave your hair pulled back and pinned up until you have finished your workout and your hair is dry from any sweat that may have formed on your scalp during the workout. Afterwards, massage in a little oil spray or spray on a little oil sheen, and finger-comb hair back to the original style. However, if your hair does get wet and is a little frizzy, a shampoo may be in order (e.g., one of the weeks in the Six-Week regimen or the Work-Out/Mid-Week Conditioning Rinse). If you can't shampoo, moisturize and go for one of the dry sets (e.g., plait, braid or twist) found in Chapter 6, and wear your hair wavy until it is time for your next shampoo. This may help avoid combing/handling while the hair may tangle easily or not be as straight as normal.

29. If for some reason your relaxer is fading before its time, (Ex. *your new growth has gotten out of control, say after five weeks instead of six weeks or longer)*, **do not relax your hair sooner than 6 weeks** (*BELIEVE ME, YOU DO NOT WANT TO DO THIS!*). The risk is too great, and *sometimes you don't see the damage for many years* – I didn't immediately notice the gradual thinning and breakage that occurred around my front right and back side edges (behind my ear) over a period of years. As a result, I thought no harm was being done as I started to relax my hair every 5-weeks. **Just because our hair looks good when it is styled does not mean that our habits are not harmful.** Damage can be done very subtly, and over time you may begin to notice dryness, excessive shedding or slower growth, which can take a lot of time and effort to reverse/correct. As a result, wait a minimum of six weeks, **but preferably 8 to 12 weeks** to avoid the danger of overlapping, which can cause your already relaxed hair, especially your edges, to be overprocessed. After consulting with a dermatologist about my own situation, I reduced the frequency of my touch-ups from every

5 weeks to every 12 – 13 weeks, longer if I can comb it without noticeable breakage. See Chapter 7 for tips on relaxing with care.

To stretch your relaxers out, try shampooing every 3-4 days to help moisturize and soften new growth (See Chapter 3 for tips). Moisturizing with **Healthier Hair in a Bottle! Oil Spray** once or twice a day (or as needed) also helps soften new growth. Wearing styles that minimize combing and handling, like updos and twist or plait/braid sets (See Chapter 6 on Styling) are also helpful. The added "nappy" factor will make crimped or wavy looks even fuller. The outcome is a different hairstyle that helps get you to the next shampoo, without damaging your hair by too much combing or brushing while your hair is in a vulnerable state. You could also braid your hair, or try twist styles, but make sure you remove braids or tight twists at least one week before you get a touch-up to avoid scalp irritation.

Chapter 6

STYLING

If I had to think of the worst hair days I have ever had, my mind would go back to the 80's, when I was in high school and college. As is often the case with young women, I was all about getting a style, not keeping my hair healthy. I spent at least 30 minutes a day, every day, curling my hair with a curling iron. However, because the curls didn't last long, I would often curl my hair again with electric/hot curlers if I went out at night. In addition to that, every time I shampooed my hair, I would blow dry it, and then I would continue with my hot curling *habit*. I had no idea that this continuous heat exposure was doing serious damage to my hair. As a result, I was always surprised and upset when I went to a salon to get a touch-up, and the stylist would trim off **ALL** of my newly acquired length after saying the words I came to dread, **S-P-L-I-T E-N-D-S!** This happened *every* time I went to the salon in the 80's, but it never occurred to me, and no one ever told me that my troubles could be caused by excessive use of heat appliances...

Because the purpose of this book is to help you have beautiful, *healthier* hair, the styles and recommendations featured in this section are low/no heat styles. While doing research for this book and trying to get my hair together, I came to the conclusion that much of the damage done to our hair is caused by: 1) the overuse of chemicals; 2) infrequent shampooing and conditioning; 3) rough handling; 4) styles that pull the hair too tightly; and 5) overuse of heat styling appliances and blow dryers. In this chapter you will find styling alternatives that can help us limit our use of heat styling tools, and there are also tips for those who might need pointers on keeping their natural styles healthy and looking good. For those of us with relaxed hair, the main goal of this chapter is to provide hairstyles and suggestions that make it easier to transition to low/no-heat styling – **without** the use of curling irons, electric curlers or flat irons. The tips provided are aimed at helping us find and wear the right balance of styles to keep our hair in top condition, while still looking good! All it takes is a little creativity, patience, practice (as you get started) and the belief that it can be done.

The Dangers of Heat Styling

Believe it or not, the way we dry and style our hair can really undermine a lot of the good work we do in our daily hair care regimen. Heating appliances may look harmless, but they can cause our hair a great deal of damage without us even realizing it. Using a curling iron on our hair is almost like putting it in an oven. As I mentioned before, I read an article in *Try It Yourself Hair* magazine (April 1998) called "Hair Facts, The Heat is On" that provided the following information from Helene Curtis Research:

The average temperature of heat appliances is 250°:

Hair Dryer	=	250°
Curling Iron	=	290°
Hot Curlers	=	220°

The study also found that 50% of all hair fibers that come in contact with heat appliances become damaged. As more evidence is found to support this, I hope to see more stylists and experts in black hair magazines showing us more examples of low/no-heat styling methods to achieve today's popular looks. Hopefully, this will happen soon so that our styles not only look good, but will be created using methods that keep our hair healthy, which is **the most important thing**. In the meantime, I will get the ball rolling with my favorite low-heat styling techniques…

Low-Heat Styling

When I use the term *low-heat styling* I am referring to any method of styling that does not involve the use of heat appliances more than 2 or 3 times a week. When heat styling tools are used, they should not be left in/on your hair for more than a few seconds (e.g., curling iron, flat iron, straightening comb, etc.). In fact, we should use these damaging items as infrequently as possible, and any alternative method must not require direct heat to be applied to our hair for long periods. With that said, I will share my favorite low-heat styling method.

The Caruso Steam Hair Setter

Although I mentioned my hair troubles of the 80's, things started looking up during the 90's. I finally threw away my curling irons and electric curlers after seeing an infomercial on BET for a new product called the Richard Caruso Molecular Steam Hair Setter (the name has since been shortened). I know it is hard to imagine, but my hair looks better, even with the occasional hair challenges, and it is healthier than it has ever been in my entire life! How was I able to do this? Well I have to give a lot of the credit to the makers of this product for giving me a healthier alternative to daily heat appliance use. Some of you may have heard of it, but very of us have been brave enough to try it. For the most part, you won't see it used/mentioned in black hair care magazines, beauty shows or salons even though it curls quicker and is less damaging than curling irons or electric curlers. I think many of the black women and styling professionals who have heard of it think that it is only for women of other ethnicities (e.g., Whites, Asians, etc.). In fact, when I first saw it, I mentioned it to one of my sisters-in-law before I bought one, and her first response was, "Steam? You'll probably wind up with an afro!" We laughed, but I was curious and motivated because I was in search of a quicker and healthier way to style my hair.

I have to admit that it does seem unbelievable that a steam product can actually work on our hair, giving long-lasting, soft curls that are the closest thing to a wet-set you can find, in a matter of minutes! Regardless, it does work, and once I figured out how to *successfully* use it on my hair, I was so pleased that I threw away all of my other heat appliances. Between using this product and then learning to air dry my hair, I saw a dramatic improvement in the overall health of my hair in a matter of months. Just two simple changes helped my hair to consistently grow past my shoulders **without** split-ends. Over the years, I have recommended this product to other women with varying hair types, and most of them experienced the same wonderful results I have.

Note: The results and recommendations described below for the Caruso Steam Hair Setter are based on experiences with relaxed hair. Although I believe the product may work on fine, natural hair with the same results as a curling iron, I cannot say that the results will be exactly the same for all types of natural hair. This is especially true for women who press/straighten their hair. The moisture from this product could cause pressed hair to revert back to its normal state. For this reason, I suggest that women with natural hair read the following section, use the tips/recommendations that apply to you, and experiment with the product to find out how well it can work for your hair.

I believe this product can revolutionize the way we curl and style our hair. The "steam" from this product adds moisture to our hair; whereas, dry heat products such as curling irons, electric curlers and blow dryers rob the hair of moisture and cause damage. Some people have expressed concern because the product uses sponge curlers, but I don't think you lose any more hair than you would during any other type of curling. Almost any time we comb our hair, we will see some shedding or broken strands – this is inevitable, but if your hair is well cared for, breakage should be very minimal, especially since you should only be using these a few times a week. One thing I can promise you is that when you use this product you will *never* smell your hair burn again, you will *never* feel metal burn your scalp or skin, and you will *never* hear your hair sizzle as you curl it! As incredible as it may sound, once I started using these curlers I never used a curling iron or electric curlers on my hair again.

Although I have heard some ladies speak of using this product on the Internet, I have yet to hear of any salons or stylists that use it. I think the problem may be that many of the ones who know about it may not know how to use it to get the results they want. I hope this changes in the future as we work toward having healthier hair, *moving away from* the popular trend of weaves, wigs and extensions. As with anything else, it takes practice to learn how to use these curlers, and then you can experiment to see how they work best for you. We had to learn how to use curling irons and electric curlers, so this is no different, except for the fact that the condition of your hair, especially the ends, will dramatically improve.

A few practice sessions may be required before you are able to use these curlers as well as you use electric curlers or curling irons. However, don't let your first time trying it be when you are getting ready for work, a big date, a special occasion or an important meeting – you don't need any pressure during your first few tries. In fact, you probably won't get your best results during the first few tries, so be prepared to try it at least five times (*on different days*) before getting frustrated. As an example, if you leave the curlers in too long or you put in too many, your head could look like an explosion of curls, and it could take a day or two for them to loosen up. Also, if you leave curlers on the heating spool too long, your curls could come out damp or a little frizzy. Remember, it took you a while to learn how to use curling irons – so *be patient*. The rewards will make it worth the effort! Before you get started, I suggest you read the directions that come with this product, *ignore the pictures in most cases*, but pay close attention to any instructions that may apply to our hair. Based on my experience using the Caruso Steam Hair Setter, I would like to *add* the following tips and recommendations:

1. Keep your hair clean by shampooing it according to the directions in Chapter 3 or a similar regimen. Curling tools work better on clean hair, and the Caruso Steam Hair Setter is no exception.

2. Do not put a lot of moisturizers/oils/creams on your hair prior to setting. Because the steam from these curlers is not damaging to your hair, I would only use a small amount of a light, rich oil such as **Healthier Hair in a Bottle! Oil Spray** or olive oil. If I use these curlers on the morning after one of my nightly/weekly ends treatments (see Chapter 5), I may not use anything on my ends before curling except for a styling wax such as **Ampro Pro-Style Marcel Wax** for a smoother finish and longer lasting curls. However, for those days where my hair is a little drier than usual, I might spray my hair and ends *lightly* with **Healthier Hair in a Bottle! Moisturizing & Detangling Mist** before detangling or finger-combing, and then smooth a little **Healthier Hair in a Bottle! Oil Spray** on the sections that are to be curled. When you use the mist and oil spray before curling, make sure you don't saturate your hair with them; otherwise, your hair could be frizzy or it might not hold curls well. To be safe you could wait a few minutes before you start. *Which products you choose to use is up to you*, but go with a styling wax at a minimum for the ends protection, hold and better looking curls.

3. To get examples of the latest hairstyles, refer to magazines such as *Sophisticate's Black Hair Styles and Care Guide, Hair Styling Trends, Hype Hair* and *Try It Yourself Hair* for ideas on styling your hair. Experiment with the Caruso Steam Hair Setter to create the same styles shown on the models in the magazines. During your experimentation, *avoid curling irons as much as possible* as you find the right styles for you. Try using

the Caruso Steam Hair Setter to create the style of your choice (e.g., curls going up for flips, etc.). First curl as you would with regular or electric curlers, and then try different curl/setting patterns to create the looks or styles of your choice. Sometimes I set my hair all over going towards the back, or I might use as few as 2 curlers going up or under. Once you get used to using this product, you will find that it gives a lot of styling versatility.

4. The Caruso Steam Hair Setter allows you to curl one section of hair at a time. While you section off a piece of hair for curling, a curler is heating on the steam unit. Do not leave the curler on the steam unit for more than a few seconds. Leaving it on too long causes water to build up in the inner chamber which can lead to drops of warm water falling on your scalp or your curls being damp. To avoid this, give the curler a quick, downward shake (with the hole in the curler toward the floor) to remove excess moisture **before** putting the curler in your hair. **This is very important:** Removing excess moisture helps prevent your curls from becoming wet, frizzy or bushy. The curlers lose their heat very quickly so try to shake them in one quick motion as you are putting the curler in your hair. The curler should be in place within 10 to 15 seconds of leaving the unit, or it may need to be reheated. If the curler should fall or lose heat, heat it again before curling or re-curling the section. This process should become easier each time you use the curlers.

5. Immediately after curling a section, while holding the curler in place in my hair, I put the cover for the curler on the steam unit for a few seconds as well. After removing it, I give it a quick shake to remove excess moisture before I put it on the curler that I am holding in my hair. Removing excess moisture helps prevent your curls from becoming wet, frizzy or bushy. The shake should be a very quick motion so that the heat is not lost. The cover should be on the curler within 5 to 10 seconds, or it may need to be reheated. If the curler and cover should fall, or if they lose heat, heat them both again and re-curl the section. The curlers do come with clips for areas that need more support, so use the clips to keep curlers from falling. Remember that it may take a few practice tries before you feel totally comfortable using them.

6. The Caruso Steam Hair Setter produces curls that are almost the same quality as a wet set. Because of this, you may not want to tightly curl a lot of small sections unless you want a *very* tight set that could take *days* to loosen up – just like a wet set. If this happens, wrapping your hair overnight can help, but I usually wear an updo for a day or two. Because the curlers come in various sizes (from petite to large), you can determine whether you want big or small curls. After experimenting you will come up with the right size and number of curlers to use to get the look you want. I very rarely use more than six of the larger curlers to set my hair – three in the front, one in the crown and two in the back. This set gives me the same results I used to get by setting my entire head with electric curlers, in less than half the time. However, the set lasts up to three times as long. The steam actually produces tighter curls that last, which means you should not have to curl your hair more than two to three times a week. Since I started using this product, I never curl my hair more than two or three times a week, and I believe this is one of the main reasons my ends have gotten a lot healthier.

The styles shown on the next page only took me 10 minutes to create – from curling to styling! It is so easy to create stylish looks for work or play. You can increase the number of curlers, change the curling pattern, create updos and twist styles, or throw on a headband for a very casual, fashionable look. These curlers give you all of the styling flexibility you could ever need, and you should not have to curl your hair for at least two to three days. This low-heat product can definitely help you grow healthier, longer hair, and once you master using it, curling irons and electric curlers will be a thing of the past!

Here are few pictures of me demonstrating the steps I just described:

Here is an example of how my hair looks after it is set, after styling and the day after…

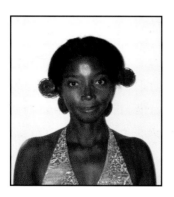  

7. After removing the curlers, I sometimes spray my hair with **Isoplus Oil Sheen Hair Spray** for extra shine, or when it is rainy or humid I *might* use **Jheri Redding Volumizer Extra Shine** *Spray-On Shine*. *Both of these products are totally optional*, and most times I don't even remember to use them. However, for the middle picture above I did use the Jheri Redding spray because it was raining like crazy as I went to have this picture taken. *So only use them if you need them.*

8. For fuller styles you can separate or tease the curls from individual sections of hair. For smoother styles, gently comb out each curl into the style of your choice (be extra careful if you used a styling wax). However, for longer lasting curls and a different look, try finger-combing or separating the curls without using a comb. These curls really last so you should not need any holding spray unless it is *very* windy. I have found that even when the wind blows my hair, the styles still easily fall back into place. So I never use hairspray, which is amazing to me seeing how my hair used to be "all over my head" anytime the wind blew!

9. For touch-ups during the day, you could lightly spray your hair with **Jheri Redding Volumizer Extra Shine** *Spray-On-Shine* or smooth on **Healthier Hair in a Bottle! Oil Spray** to give extra shine.

10. Still wear a satin cap/scarf or thin plastic cap at night to preserve the curls the same as you would with any other style.

If you are a frequent heat styler (using curling irons or electric curlers more than three times a week), the Caruso Steam Hair Setter may be one of the best things you can add to your daily regimen. If you make a small investment of time to learn how to use it best for your length and style, you will be able to throw away your curling irons and electric curlers, like I did. You may not see the results on your hair immediately, but in a matter of months you could see a **BIG** difference in your hair's condition and length. Not only will this help save your hair, but you can also cut your weekly setting and styling time in half! Try it, I think you will be impressed.

Natural Styling - Pressing/Hot Combing/Straightening

I remember when my hair was natural as a little girl I had a love-hate relationship with my mother's straightening comb. I used to love wearing bangs and any chance at having my hair hang loose was welcomed, especially if I could get any kind of Shirley Temple curls going. However, I hated the time it took to have my thick, air dried hair combed through and straightened. I remember it was usually a hot day, my mother would comb my hair roughly and quickly, and worst of all, not only did it take forever, but I also usually got a burn on at least one ear. My mother would start at the back, and because I sweat so much, by the time she got to the front, the back of my neck was *"beaded"* up again. These are not good memories, but I must admit, in hindsight they were a lot better than the ones I have of my earliest relaxer experiences. *The occasional burn on the ear is not as hard to recover from as a poorly applied relaxer*, and pressing is temporary – it won't take years to transition from it if you decide you don't like it. So for those reasons, I think pressing or straightening is a great alternative for women who want to occasionally wear straight styles and revert back to natural styles whenever they want, without the chemicals and without the hassle.

So if you think pressing is for you, here are a few tips that may help ensure that you have a good experience:

1. As the name of this section implies, you should only press/straighten *natural* hair (hair that is not relaxed or texturized). I know sometimes it seems like it would be harmless, especially if you are close to needing a touch-up, but it is not – it can lead to *serious* breakage.

2. If you are not trained in pressing/straightening, or you don't feel comfortable doing it yourself, you should visit a stylist that has been trained to do this. I would also suggest checking out some of their customers beforehand, if possible.

3. Your hair should be clean and well-conditioned (can be achieved by performing the steps in the Six-Week regimen) *before* pressing. It should also be completely dry before you start.

4. Separate your hair into at least 4 sections, and moisturize it with a rich oil and/or a pressing wax like **Ampro Pro Styl Marcel Wax**, especially the ends and edges **before** using a hot comb on it. *Never straighten/press your hair without moisturizing it first.*

5. Buy a good quality comb, with smooth teeth. Always make sure your comb is in good working order **before** you start. If it looks as though it can snag or catch on your hair, don't use it. *One thing you certainly don't need is a hot comb stuck in your hair!*

6. Test your comb **before** it touches your hair, making sure it is not too hot. If you are not careful, you could scorch or burn strands of hair, and if you burn them badly enough, they will break off. I have seen some people use a towel to test it beforehand. Also, limit the amount of time the hot comb is in your hair – do not run it through a section more than once or twice.

7. Be especially careful when straightening close to your scalp, burns can cause long-term scalp damage. To help avoid this, you may want to hold off on oiling your scalp until after pressing/straightening.

8. Regardless of how long your hair remains straight from pressing, *try not to press it more often than once every other week.* Even if your hair reverts back, you should still wait as long as you can. Otherwise, you could experience heat damage. Try updos or plait/twist/braid sets while you wait. Also, as you shampoo your hair during this time, if you want to wear straighter styles, try blow drying (see Chapter 4) with temporary straightening leave-ins (e.g., Lottabody, Bone Strait, etc.).

9. Try to use curling irons/appliances as rarely as possible – natural hair can still be damaged by excessive heat. In addition to heat styling, you can also do some of the dry sets shown later in this chapter (e.g., overnight twist, braid, plait and wrap sets). This will help keep pressing/straightening a form of "low-heat" styling and minimize your risk for heat damage.

10. Just like with relaxed hair, pressed/straightened hair should be handled with care (e.g., minimal combing and brushing, daily moisturizing and protection at night, etc.).

11. You can find additional tips by doing a search on the Internet. There are a number of sites that cater to natural hair. You can do a search on words like "pressing", "straightening", "natural hair", etc.

No-Heat Styling

While I love using the Caruso Steam Hair Setter to create lots of different looks, and I think it is a healthier alternative than curling irons and electric curlers, I must admit that *styles that do not require any heat at all are definitely healthier.* Surprisingly, there are many wonderful styles that women of color can create without the use of heat, whether their hair is natural or relaxed – braids, cornrows, locks, twists, wraps and curly styles. There is so much we can do to keep our hair looking stylish while **healthy**, regardless of our hair type. This section will give you tips on achieving some of the most common no-heat styles that will save you time and keep your hair as healthy as possible.

Braids, Cornrows, Locks & Twists

When I was a little girl, I used to love to get my hair braided. I loved the different styles and patterns some talented sisters could create with little strands of hair – the left side could be going down to the side, the right side could be going towards the back, and the hair in the back could be braided in a circle, and all of this could happen in the same hairstyle! Now that is versatility! I think that is the beauty of natural styling, *unlimited styling options*, with none of the dangers of harsh chemicals. So if I realize this, how did I become a relaxer user, and sometimes abuser? Well, when I hit my teenage years, I *realized* how large my head was (with a little help from my friends and family, of course) and how braided styles kinda made this even more obvious. So having relatively straight hair that I could curl was a way to frame/hide my face – a teenage coping mechanism that carried over into adulthood. Also, more importantly, I am lazy and do not have the patience to sit down for hours to let someone braid my hair, no matter how beautiful the result might be. Regardless, I do appreciate the beauty of these styles on other women, *especially when it is their own hair.*

Even as I admire these styles on other sisters, I do notice that some struggle to maintain these styles – just as we who choose to relax struggle to maintain ours. Because of this, I would like to offer some tips I have run across over the years on keeping natural styles looking their best, while keeping the hair and scalp healthy as it can be.

1. Be very selective when selecting braiders and natural stylists. Try to see examples of their work *in person* **before** using them – look to see how tight braids are done and look at the person's edges to see if they actually have any, and try to get an idea of the type of stress the stylist put on them. The goal is to pick one good stylist, and try to stick with them if possible. *You really can't be too careful.* A number of dermatologists have begun to express concern about the long-term damage *we* are doing to our scalps as we wear some of the most popular braided and natural styles (e.g., receding hair lines, bald spots, etc.). Once that hair is gone, it is almost impossible to get it back the way it was, especially when hair is pulled out from the root or the follicles are damaged. Too many times warning signs are overlooked, and we don't see damage until it is too late. So you definitely want to find a stylist who realizes the possible damage that can be caused if these styles are not done properly and who is committed to keeping your hair and scalp healthy as well as giving you a stylish look.

2. Wait a few weeks after relaxing your hair before braiding, cornrowing or twisting. Relaxing our hair temporarily weakens it, and the straighter it is, the less elasticity it will have (the less it will stretch). The less elasticity a strand of hair has, the quicker it will break, and because the process of braiding, cornrowing and twisting can involve a lot of pulling on individual sections of hair, not waiting could lead to unnecessary breakage. In addition to waiting, I would also suggest that you start off with clean, well-conditioned hair as you get these types of styles.

3. The reverse of the tip above is not to relax your hair immediately after having braids, cornrows, locks or twists removed, especially if you have had them in for a while (longer than 4 or 5 weeks). I say this because even though you are not actually combing your hair when you have these styles, there is constant stress on your scalp from having your hair pulled in a style that does not change for long periods, especially if you have any kind of extensions. As a result, *you should try to wait at least 2 weeks after having your braided or twisted styles removed before chemically treating your hair.* I know this may seem like a long time, but it is just a precaution to make sure your scalp has time to recover from any irritation or stress caused by your natural style, minimizing any increased risk for damage from the relaxer. During the rest period, you should shampoo and deep condition and wear a much looser style such as a plait, braid or twist set (described later in this chapter) to give your scalp a much needed rest.

4. When selecting a style, keep in mind that some are healthier than others, and as a result, there are some that should not be done on a regular basis. One of those is microbraids – your hair is almost guaranteed to experience breakage unless the person putting them in is **extremely careful**, especially around the hairline. Another is any style that uses thick, heavy braided extensions and/or ornaments – go for the lightest weight and size braid you can for the style you are trying to create. The goal is to put as little stress on individual sections of your hair as you can. You should also make sure you don't put in too many braids or beaded ornaments. Otherwise, it is difficult for your scalp to breathe and for you to moisturize the scalp below them. Finally, don't pull braids into tight pony-tails for long periods. This is just added stress to an already stressful style – your hair line could suffer, not to mention your scalp in general if you do this too often.

5. I know many stylists say that you can leave braids/cornrows, locks and twists in for 6-8 weeks, or longer, but I think that many dermatologists would agree that this could be too long for the average person's scalp. Having your hair in the same style, with stress on the same sections of hair for long periods, can cause thinning and baldness in areas of your scalp as well as a receding hair line, **especially with microbraids**. Not that I personally have anything against these types of braids, but I have seen and heard of the damage they can cause, especially in young girls who are starting to suffer from thinning and hair-loss conditions typically found in middle-aged women. This is really sad because damage can be avoided with a little preventive maintenance, and the acknowledgement that *no one, whether the hair is natural or relaxed, should wear the same hair style for months on end if it puts any kind of stress on the scalp*. Even if it doesn't put stress on your scalp, your hair is slowly drying out and matting, which could lead to tangling nightmares when you finally decide to take it down, which means unnecessary breakage.

6. Some stylists recommend wiping your hairline with a cotton ball lightly soaked with Witch Hazel or Sea Breeze Astringent to minimize tightness and bumps. However, if you find that you still feel tightness or pain around your hairline after a few days or see bumps, you should **go back to your stylist as soon as possible to have any section(s) causing you pain redone**. If you feel unnecessary pulling, stress on a section or worse, pain, *this could be an area where you will have problems in the future with thinning or balding*, and if a stylist values you as a customer, he/she will do what is necessary for the health of your scalp. Even if they don't want to, you need to be concerned enough to make sure they do. Otherwise, *find someone else who will*.

7. If your hair is braided or cornrowed, and you see or suspect thinning in a section(s) of your hair, you may want to alternate the direction of your braids or cornrows (e.g., instead of them all going back, maybe one section can go to the side, etc.). If you can't change the style up, you may need to change the style altogether. Whatever you decide, you cannot afford to ignore early warning signs that your hair and/or scalp may give you – if you see a thin/bald patch, *there is a problem*, and you need to find the cause and fix it *before it is too late*. I see too many people, even celebrities, where their hairlines have receded inch after inch, year after year, yet they are still wearing the same style. We all have to be proactive in preventing damage – just because we like a style, we cannot be afraid to change something that is not working. Remember, one of the beauties of wearing braids and other natural styles is the flexibility in your styling options, and a trained stylist should be able to help you find healthier alternatives.

8. In addition to the previous tip, I must add that even though having a trained stylist can **help**, you should not rely on them entirely to tell you if you are having a problem with your scalp or hair. I say this because unfortunately many of them may not be trained, may not care enough, or may not take the time to look for warning signs relating to the overall health of your scalp – many of them are only *trained to style*. For many stylists, braiding, cornrowing, twisting and locking hair is their livelihood, and often they are in a rush or distracted when you are getting your hair done. I do believe that responsible, well-trained stylists should be able to assess your situation and advise you, but in the real world, I just don't think you can take this for

granted. I say this because you may think that your hairline is receding a bit, but you are not sure, and so you justify it in your mind by saying, "well, if I had a problem, my stylist would have noticed/mentioned it, right?" Maybe, but **maybe not**. *Identifying problems is ultimately our responsibility.* I feel strongly about this tip because I thought I noticed thinning around my edges, but I dismissed it at first because *my stylist never mentioned it.* I was thinking that if I had a problem she would **surely** notice and tell me first. Well, she didn't, and the overprocessing that was going on in my case continued for years longer than it should have. Was it her fault? To a certain extent, but who was left kicking herself? *Me* – so the lesson I learned was, "my hair, my responsibility!" So, bottom line tip for you, "**your hair, your responsibility!**"

9. Avoid adding synthetic hair pieces to your natural styles – they can dry your natural hair out and potentially lead to unnecessary dryness and breakage.

10. For those of you wanting styling ideas for natural hair, there are so many sites and hair boards on the web now that provide styles for all of us – even for those of us with relaxed hair who want to wear the styles temporarily. These sites are really a blessing because women can exchange ideas relating to specific problems they have encountered and alternate styles/regimens that they have come up with. Because no one has the perfect, end-all-be-all hair care or styling solution for everyone's hair, these sources can provide valuable information to supplement your regimen. They can also offer help to those wanting to transition from relaxed hair. A few of the ones I have heard of are www.nasabb.com/nasabbnew/hairtips.htm, www.sisterlocks.com, www.treasuredlocks.com, www.growafrohairlong.com, www.nappturality.com, and www.nappyhair.com/styles/styles.htm. However, doing a search on the Internet as well as checking out magazines that showcase these styles might provide others.

Twist Sets

This no-heat set can be used to create a look that is a cross between a crimp and a spiral set. It is a great style when you want a texturized or wavy look or when you want to wear an updo with loose curls hanging in the front, back or on the sides. This set can be used on all types of hair, with varying degrees of curls based on the texture of your hair. **Note:** It may be difficult to go back to a straight style or regular curls after doing this set, *without shampooing first, but you can create really interesting updos, twists and buns.* To create this set:

1. Work a small amount of **Healthier Hair in a Bottle! Moisturizing & Detangling Mist** or wrapping/setting lotion through the hair to moisturize, add body or give extra hold (both products are optional). Then finger-comb hair to the back.

2. Part hair in equal sections (I sometimes do 4, 2 in the front, and 2 in the back) and smooth on a little **Healthier Hair in a Bottle! Oil Spray** to each section. The number of sections you choose is up to you, sometimes I have done only 1 or 2, which gives much looser curls. However, to make the set last longer and the crimps tighter, make smaller sections. Starting with 1 section at a time, twist from the scalp to the ends. Once firmly twisted, take the end and wrap it around the base of the section (at the scalp), tucking the end of the hair under the wrapped hair.

3. Use one or two bobby/hair pins to secure each section. If your ends remain tucked under, the pins are optional.

4. If you are doing this overnight, you can cover your hair with a satin cap/scarf or thin plastic cap before bed if you wish. However, if I am sleeping on my satin pillow cover, I usually don't wear a cap.

5. When the set has been in place for at least 4 hours, remove the pins and untwist sections. Separate each section with your fingers, and finger-comb as needed. Do not use a comb unless you want to loosen curls.

6. If your hair had any curl to it when this set was performed, the ends may already have a natural curl that makes it look as though they have been curled under. However, if you would like to "bump" your ends to make them curl under more, use a few Caruso curlers (pick the largest size that fits) on large sections of your ends. You don't want the curls to be too tight, so loosely curl sections, and remove the curlers after a few minutes. As you wear this style, you can experiment with the size and number of curlers, as well as how long to leave them in to create different looks. *If you choose not to curl or bump the ends, you may want to put a little **Healthier Hair in a Bottle! Ends Treatment**, **Vaseline** or styling wax on the ends to make them look a little more polished and less prone to frizz*

7. Spray your hair lightly with **Isoplus Oil Sheen Hair Spray** or rub on a small amount of **Healthier Hair in a Bottle! Oil Spray** or **Fantasia IC Hair Polisher**, especially if it is humid or wet outside. For extra shine and frizz protection, I have also sprayed on a small amount of **Jheri Redding Volumizer Extra Shine** *Spray-On-Shine.* All of this is optional, *only use the products you feel you need.*

Before:

& After:

Maintenance Tip: *To get these looks to last longer, you can spritz sections with* **Healthier Hair in a Bottle! Moisturizing & Detangling Mist** *or a little tap water, then smooth on a little* **Healthier Hair in a Bottle! Oil Spray***, and "re-twist" your hair overnight and pin each section. You can bump the ends in the morning if you want more curl. After 2 or 3 days, you may need to start "recycling" the style through the use of an updo or pony-tail. Here are a few examples:*

These styles are a major blessing if you need to shampoo your hair at night, and you want something different and low maintenance.

Additional Tips:

- The more twists you do, the greater the risk for tangling. The most I would do is 5, 2 in the front, with a middle part, 1 in the crown, and 2 in the back with a middle part, which makes it easier to sleep on my back. However, to avoid tangling, **the fewer you do, the better**.

- If you encounter a tangle, do not try to pull the tangled strands apart. Instead, gently smooth the strands down to the very ends with your fingers, put a little **Healthier Hair in a Bottle! Moisturizing & Detangling Mist** on the tangled section, and slowly separate the individual strands. If you try to pull the strands apart before straightening them to their full length, you run a greater risk of breaking multiple strands and leaving frizzy-looking ends. Even though this style is quick and low-maintenance, it still requires you to take a great deal of care when separating sections, initially and during touch-up styling.

- When taking the pins out, instead of unraveling the twists and separating the sections, gently separate the sections while the twist is still "twisted". For some reason, if I try to unravel it before separating, it seems to tangle more. However, if I spray a little oil on it and just start separating it as soon as I unwrap the section from around the base, there are less tangles. As I said before, the fewer twists you do, the less risk of tangling, but regardless of how many you do, you have to take your time as you untwist.

- After you separate all of the twists, you may look in the mirror and think, "*What a mess!*" I have this thought every time I do this set! The secret to getting it to look good is to finger comb the loosened sections, and apply oil to the ends/hair as needed. As you finger-comb, play with it to see which direction you want the hair to fall. It will look better and fuller as you continue to separate/finger-comb, and your finished look can still look pretty decent up to the 3rd or 4th day.

- You can leave the ends straight or bump them with Caruso curlers. However, if you see any frizz or if your ends don't look as smooth as you would like, you can make them look more polished by smoothing a little **Healthier Hair in a Bottle! Ends Treatment** or **Vaseline** on them.

- Some have asked if I do a comb-out before shampooing out a twist set, but I have to say that I never do. Most times the curls are loosened as I rinse my hair in the shower before I even put the shampoo on it. By the time I finish shampooing, my hair is completely straight. The KeraCare shampoo and conditioner I recommend in the Six-Week Regimen are great products for detangling.

Plait/Braid Sets

This is another no-heat, overnight set that is great when you want a texturized or wavy look or when you want to wear an updo with loose curls hanging in the front, back or on the sides. This set provides a look comparable to the twist set, but there is a more pronounced crimp, although less curl, in the hair. The longer you leave the hair plaited/braided, the more pronounced the crimps will be and the longer they will last, so depending on the look you want, you can wear this set to bed overnight or when you are working around the house. This set can be used on all types of hair, with varying degrees of curls based on the texture of your hair. **Note:** It may be difficult to go back to a straight style or regular curls after doing this set, *without shampooing first, but you can create really interesting updos, twists and buns.*

To create this set:

1. Work a small amount of **Healthier Hair in a Bottle! Moisturizing & Detangling Mist** or wrapping/setting lotion through the hair to moisturize, add body or give extra hold (both of these products are optional). Then finger-comb hair to the back.

2. Part hair and section it. Smooth on a little **Healthier Hair in a Bottle! Oil Spray** to each section. The number of sections you choose is up to you. Sometimes I have done only one or two, which gives much looser curls. In this case, I say as many as you feel like plaiting/braiding. However, to make the set last longer and the crimps tighter, make smaller sections. The smaller the sections, the fuller the style will be. Starting with one section at a time, plait/braid hair from the scalp to the ends. Continue plaiting/braiding sections until your entire head is plaited/braided.

3. If you are doing this overnight, you can cover your hair with a satin cap/scarf or thin plastic cap before bed if you wish. However, if I am sleeping on my satin pillow cover, I usually don't wear a cap.

4. When the set has been in place for at least 4 hours, loosen or undo the plaits/braids.

5. Separate each section with your fingers, and finger-comb as needed. Do not use a regular comb unless you want to loosen the curls.

6. If your hair had any curl to it when this set was performed, the ends may already have a natural curl that makes it look as though they have been curled under. However, if you would like to "bump" your ends to make them curl under more, use a few Caruso curlers (pick the largest size that fits) on large sections of your ends. You don't want the curls to be too tight, so loosely curl sections, and remove the curlers after a few minutes. As you wear this style, you can experiment with the size and number of curlers, as well as how long to leave them in to create different looks. *If you choose not to curl or bump the ends, you may want to put a little **Healthier Hair in a Bottle! Ends Treatment, Vaseline** or styling wax on the ends to make them look a little more polished and less prone to frizz.* **Note:** *You can use any type of soft curler overnight instead of the Caruso curlers.*

7. Spray your hair lightly with **Isoplus Oil Sheen Hair Spray,** and/or rub on a small amount of **Healthier Hair in a Bottle! Oil Spray** or **Fantasia IC Hair Polisher**, especially if it is humid or wet outside. For extra shine

and frizz protection, I have also sprayed on a small amount of **Jheri Redding Volumizer Extra Shine *Spray-On-Shine***. *All of this is optional, only use products you feel you need.*

Before & After:

Maintenance Tip: *To get these looks to last longer, you can spritz sections with* **Healthier Hair in a Bottle! Moisturizing & Detangling Mist** *or a little tap water, then smooth on a little* **Healthier Hair in a Bottle! Oil Spray**, *and "re-plait" or "re-braid" your hair overnight. You can bump the ends in the morning if you want more curl. However, most people can only extend this set 2 or 3 days. After this time, you may need to start "recycling" the style through the use of an updo or pony-tail.*

The "Night-On-The-Town" Quick Set

This option is great for special occasions (or even work) where you have no time to do your hair or you want something different and versatile in 30 minutes or less. With an old trick from the past, you can have the almost exact look as the plait/braid set from above, in a fraction of the time. Following the steps below will allow you to create a texturized or wavy look – loose and free flowing or an updo with loose curls hanging in the front, back or on the sides. This set can be used on all types of hair, with varying degrees of curls based on the texture of your hair. **Note:** *I recommend trying this set a few days before you are scheduled to shampoo your hair because this set, usually, can only be washed out. Most women cannot go back to a straight style or regular curls, without shampooing first, but you can create really interesting updos, twists and buns as the waves wear out.*

To create this set:

1. Work a small amount of **Healthier Hair in a Bottle! Moisturizing & Detangling Mist,** wrapping/setting lotion or water through the hair to moisturize, add body or give extra hold. Then finger-comb hair to the back.

2. Part hair in 2-inch sections or smaller depending on how tight or long-lasting you want the crimp or curl to be, and smooth on a little **Healthier Hair in a Bottle! Oil Spray** to each section. The number of sections you choose is up to you, but the more you do, and the smaller the sections are, the fuller the style will be and the longer it will last. I usually do as many as I have time to plait (e.g., 1, 2, 4 or 6).

3. Plait/braid each section (you could also do twists) from the scalp to the ends. If you want more curl, you could also put in some curlers on the plaited/braided sections.

4. When you are done, take a shower, do your make-up, get dressed or whatever you need to do while you **air dry your hair for approximately 15-30 minutes.** To shorten the time you could also dry the braids/plaits with a blow dryer (no attachment needed) or sit under a hooded dryer.

5. When the plaits/braids or twists are dry, remove any curlers you may have added first, and undo the plaits/braids or twists.

6. Separate each section with your fingers, and finger-comb as needed. Do not use a comb unless you want to loosen the curls.

7. If your hair had any curl to it when this set was performed, the ends may already have a natural curl that makes it look as though they have been curled under. However, if you would like to "bump" your ends to make them curl under more, use a few Caruso curlers (pick the largest size that fits) on large sections of your ends. You don't want the curls to be too tight, so loosely curl sections, and remove the curlers after a few minutes. *If you choose not to curl or bump the ends, you may want to put a little **Healthier Hair in a Bottle! Ends Treatment**, **Vaseline** or styling wax on the ends to make them look a little more polished and less prone to frizz.*

8. After removing the curlers or undoing the plaits/braids or twists, you can spray your hair lightly with **Isoplus Oil Sheen Hair Spray,** or rub on a small amount of **Healthier Hair in a Bottle! Oil Spray** or **Fantasia IC Hair Polisher**, especially if it is humid or wet outside. For extra shine and frizz protection, I have also sprayed on a small amount of **Jheri Redding Volumizer Extra Shine *Spray-On-Shine.*** *All of this is optional, only use products you feel you need.*

9. To get the "baby hair" look, you can also add a little **Vaseline** and water to your edges or curl activator (e.g., Long Aid, etc.), and smooth gently with a brush. Then you are truly all set for whatever the evening or day holds for you!

Maintenance Tip: *To get this look to last longer "re-wet", moisturize and "re-plait" your hair overnight and sleep in a satin cap/scarf or on a satin pillow cover. Bump the ends in the morning as necessary.*

Wrap Sets

Hair wrapping is a technique that provides you with sleek, straight styles, with a lot of body and bounce. Wrap sets can be done on all lengths of hair, dry or wet. When the hair is *unwrapped*, it can be worn straight or you can "bump" the ends to give them some curl. Until you have done this set a couple of times it can be very tricky to master. Even today, if I am not careful, I have to rewrap my hair all over again to get it right. My stylist taught me to "wrap" by first wrapping her hair and allowing me to watch. She then wrapped mine and instructed me as I wrapped my own. If you have never "wrapped" hair, you might want to get your stylist to demonstrate the technique using your hair or someone else's to help you get the hang of it. The directions shown below will make more sense if you already have an idea of how a wrap is done. To wrap hair, follow the steps below:

Note: *When you are finished, your hair will look like a beehive, similar to a 60's bouffant hairdo, with a hollow center at the top.*

1. Rub a small amount of **Healthier Hair in a Bottle! Oil Spray** onto your hair (especially the ends) and **detangle** by combing or finger-combing your hair to the back. You could also use a little wrapping lotion like (e.g., Nu Expressions, Lottabody, etc.) for extra hold.

2. Decide which direction you want your hair to hang or fall. Then make a part on the opposite side of your head, in the front of your hair. You are going to wrap the hair in the opposite direction of the way you want the hair to hang or fall.

3. After you make the part, start smoothing the hair in the direction opposite of the direction you want it to hang or fall. Use a wide-tooth comb to gently comb/smooth the hair from the side of the part towards the back of the neck. Continue smoothing until the hair lays flat. You can use a soft brush to gently smooth the hair. Make sure the length of your hair has been smoothed over as far as it can go (for medium and shoulder length hair, that is resting on your opposite shoulder).

4. Next, part a small, diagonal section starting from the part in the front of your hair. **While holding the palm of your hand on the top of your head** (*very important* – to keep the loose hair from being pulled with the section you are wrapping), comb/brush this section around the already wrapped hair that is resting at the base of your neck. Use a comb to gently rake the hair until it rests flat and smooth on top of the already wrapped hair.

5. Repeat step 4 until only a small section of hair is left (only the hair resting at the base of your neck should remain). After wrapping a couple of sections, gently smooth or tighten the wrap with a brush.

6. Take the remaining section and comb or brush it around the already wrapped hair. Use your hands or a brush to smooth and tighten the wrap. You can also rub on a little oil as you smooth your hair in the direction of the wrap.

7. Place bobby pins in front and behind both ears to keep the wrap in place.

8. Cover hair with a satin cap/scarf, or you can leave it out if you sleep on a satin pillow cover.

9. When the set has been in place for at least 6 to 8 hours, remove the pins and gently unwrap hair using your fingers or a brush to smooth.

10. Your hair will have a natural curl that makes it look as though the ends have been curled under. However, if you would like to "bump" your ends or add volume to your crown, use Caruso curlers (pick the largest size that will fit) on large sections of your hair. As you wear this style on a regular basis, you can experiment with the size and number of curlers, where to put them as well as how long to leave them in to create different looks.

11. Next, spray hair lightly with **Isoplus Oil Sheen Hair Spray,** or rub on a small amount of **Fantasia IC Hair Polisher** or **Healthier Hair in a Bottle! Oil Spray**. When the weather is humid or wet, you could also spray on a small amount of **Jheri Redding Volumizer Extra Shine *Spray-On-Shine***. *All of these products are optional, only use the ones you actually need.*

Here are a few examples of me wrapping my hair along with styles I have been able to create:

Before:

After:

Other Setting Options

One day while shopping in a beauty supply store, I ran across a product called *Hair Twirlers*. The product was advertised as "A new twist in hair design", and being the sucker that I am, I bought it. For those of you over 30, the "Twirlers" look like a product from the 80's called *Benders* (a product not designed for "us" that claimed to give curly or wavy looks). I bought a set of *Benders* too, and threw them away after I could not get them to do for me what they did for the white women in the pictures that came with it. Well, unlike that product, the Hair Twirlers are not heated and gave pretty good results. I have found other interesting setting products like *Solar Rollers by Nandi, Conair Soft Curlers, Pillow Soft Rollers by Goody* and *Designed for Me Stylers by Velcro* to name a few. My mind has been completely opened where curling our hair is concerned, especially after seeing my sister-in-law set a family member's hair with torn pieces of a paper bag, and the end result actually looked good! *Contrary to popular belief, we don't always need to use heat or spend a lot of money to look good!*

Sometimes we assume that various setting tools may not work for us because we have never used them before or because the pictures for them show white women. However, in the interest of limiting our hair's exposure to heat, we are going to have to overlook pictures and start experimenting – that is how I got most of the information contained in this book. Without taking a chance, I never would have run across the Caruso Steam Hair Setter. Some of the pictures on these products may be dated and comical, but you can use them and the product directions to give you ideas or examples on how you can set your hair during the day or overnight. The few times I have been brave enough to try these styling/setting alternatives I started off with *damp* hair, *not sopping wet* but from air drying a few hours after a shampoo or a light spritzing of **Healthier Hair in a Bottle! Moisturizing and Detangling Mist.** Then I set my hair on products like I mentioned above. It took less than an hour to set by air drying (*this time will vary, depending on how quickly your hair dries and how wet it was when you set it*). I know it sounds unbelievable, but there was no heat, it was quick and easy, and in most cases, my hair had a curly/wavy look, with loose, flexible curls. You can try any of these setting tools to create many different looks. However, to do a basic set using any of the products mentioned, you can use the following steps as a guideline:

1. Work a small amount of **Healthier Hair in a Bottle! Moisturizing & Detangling Mist** or setting/wrapping through the hair to moisturize, add body or give extra hold. *These products are optional.* Then finger-comb hair to the back.

2. Part hair in equal sections, and smooth on a little **Healthier Hair in a Bottle! Oil Spray** to each section. The number of sections you choose is up to you. Determine whether you want small, medium or large curls – tight or loose, and select the appropriate size/product.

3. Curl or set each section as described in your product's directions (if applicable) or as you see fit. If you are using a product that is not actually a curler (e.g., Hair Twirlers, Solar Curlers, etc.), curl hair around the setting item (e.g., paper bag, Hair Twirler, etc.), and wind it until you reach the scalp. Then bend the ends of your product toward each other at the front of the curl, and pin as needed. Experiment to determine the best method for your hair.

4. When the set has been in place for at least 30 minutes to an hour, check for dryness before removing the curling accessories. Sitting under a dryer for 5 to 10 minutes can shorten the time needed for your hair to set, especially if your hair was damp to start with. Also, if the curling appliances used are *very soft and do not put any stress on your scalp,* you could even do this set overnight.

5. Separate each section with your fingers, and finger-comb as needed. Do not use a regular comb unless you want to loosen curls.

6. Next, spray hair lightly with **Isoplus Oil Sheen Hair Spray,** or rub on a small amount of **Fantasia IC Hair Polisher** or **Healthier Hair in a Bottle! Oil Spray**. When the weather is humid or wet, you could also spray on a small amount of **Jheri Redding Volumizer Extra Shine *Spray-On-Shine.*** All of these products are optional, use only the ones you actually need.

Chapter 7

RELAXING WITH CARE...

As I approach the big 4-0 (40!), I would say I definitely have developed a love-hate relationship with relaxers. I have been relaxing my hair ever since I was about 10 years old. A lady in the neighborhood did my first one, and I don't remember it being too pretty – my hair was barely straight, it was somewhere in between relaxed and natural (not quite either), and it felt dry most of the time. I was told to grease my scalp with Ultra Sheen grease, and we probably washed it every few weeks because of all the trouble it took to get it looking half-way decent again. I ran for cover when it rained. I didn't want to be anywhere near a pool if people were splashing, and if I wanted my hair to look decent, I didn't do too many things that made me sweat. It was a terrible time, and I have the pictures to prove it! I can see why many sisters who grew up with a similar experience, or saw someone who did, decide to go natural!

Why Bother?

Sometimes you have to wonder why many of us bother! I did, and still do it, for the convenience. I do not know how to braid/cornrow, and my hair was very hard to manage even when it was in that *in-between* state, where it wasn't totally straight and it wasn't totally kinky. My mom and I had no idea what to do with a pre-teen/teen-age girl's hair in terms of styling, so a lot of times I either wore curlers at night, kept it in a pony-tail or got cornrows/braids. So for any of you who might have known me, growing up in Underwood Homes of Augusta, GA, your memories of me have to include recollections of a bookworm, with glasses and messed up hair filled with tuck combs, and to think my mom actually paid someone to do my hair!

Prior to relaxers I used to get my natural hair pressed/straightened, but because I sweat profusely as soon as temps get past 80 degrees, by the time you get to the front, the back of my hair would already be "peasy" again. For the most part, it was a complete waste of time. Back then, many of us viewed a "perm" as being the answer to all of our hair problems – I know I did! However, over 25 years later, I realize that what I will now call *"relaxer abuse"* led me down a path of countless avoidable hair ailments: slow growth, split-ends, dryness, breakage, thinning, etc. Looking around, *I know I am not by myself*! Many of us are overly dependent on relaxers without even realizing it. Even being armed with a little knowledge, I know I had started to mistake dryness of my new growth and ends for being in need of a touch-up. I didn't realize, *nor did my stylist*, that due to diet, age or whatever, my hair had started to get a little drier. As it turns out, ***it needed to be moisturized and shampooed more frequently, not relaxed more***. Also, because I was just getting in the real swing of a hair care regimen that finally worked, and my hair was noticeably growing, I was so excited to see progress with each touch-up that next thing I know, I was relaxing every 5-6 weeks, instead of every 6 weeks. This was the beginning of **major** *foolishness* in my regimen. Isn't it funny that the results you work so hard for can be undone or reduced by one simple thing – okay, so relaxers are not "simple", but you know what I mean!

To Relax Or Not To Relax?

Even though you might have your own sad story to share, many of us are still not prepared to give up relaxing our hair. To be honest, when I take care of my hair, I like the way my relaxed hair looks. Not that there is anything wrong with natural styles, but I prefer wearing my hair straight most of the times, which means I have to be prepared to do what is required to keep it healthy. Some people try to make the choice of natural vs. relaxed a philosophical debate – maybe it is, but I believe it is a sister's own personal choice. I have heard some say that women who relax have been brainwashed into a Eurocentric way of thinking about beauty – I don't know and don't even want to get into that debate! I am not that deep in my thinking, I just know what I like, and I am now willing to accept the responsibility of caring for hair that may be damaged by my personal choices or oversight. So not only do we as black women have choices, but ***we do have a responsibility to take the best care of our hair that we know how to regardless of how we choose to wear it.***

Believe it or not, I actually thought about going natural this summer – *I don't think I was serious though, just really fed up*. I was frustrated and disillusioned with the results of my last few touch-up appointments. I have been complaining to my stylist about the thinning and breakage that occurred around my front and side edges, which I can see improvement and signs of recovery – that is *until I get another touch-up*. With the improvements in my regimen, the use of Healthier Hair in a Bottle! Oil Spray, and waiting 12-13 weeks before a touch-up, I see hair filling in and growing longer, but as soon as my stylist does a touch-up **and** puts in semi-permanent color to cover my gray, I see patchiness, and what could still be breakage or slow growth. There are some areas (the back sides, behind my ears) that are only a third of my hair's longest length. At first I attributed it to the 5-week relaxer schedule I sank to, but then I started going almost 2 ½ times as long, so what was the problem? I then started wondering if some of it could be caused by the fact that we weren't getting all of the relaxer rinsed out because my stylist had started coming to my house (a luxury that I grew to love), and she would shampoo my hair in my kitchen sink. My problem areas were coincidentally the areas that are hardest to reach. In addition to that,

I noticed that my scalp now burns pretty quickly with the relaxer my stylist uses although it is *supposedly* a "mild" version of a popular relaxer for sensitive scalps (I won't mention the name). However, there are some areas around my front edges that felt burned or irritated after my last touch-up. Needless to say I have been very disheartened about the whole matter, and often I wish that I was trained to apply chemicals myself! You find a stylist that you like on a personal level, but your gut is telling you there is a problem... I walked away from my last appointment knowing that it was time for me to make a change... Even armed with tips and information, I admit that this is scary, especially if you don't like change, which I don't (*I force myself to do what is required though*).

Other Options

My "change" mentality was fueled even more by a recent visit to my mother. I was surprised and saddened to see her looking like the *Heat Mizer* from one of my favorite Christmas cartoons ("The Year Without a Santa Claus"). I asked her what happened, and she told me that she got a touch-up at a family member's house, and the person was talking so much that it seemed like she didn't shampoo and rinse her hair as long as she should have. However, *my mother never said anything*. By the next day, pieces of hair started breaking off as my mother ran her fingers through it. Last time I saw her it looked nice and was a little below her ears. However, now the hair in the front and back was *all broken off – uneven and short*. "Some" of the middle was her old length, and it was sticking straight up, and it was kinda reddish brown, instead of dark brown/black. IT WAS TERRIBLE! MY MOTHER WAS A SIGHT, and she was talking about going to a family member's wedding in a few days, and she wanted to look good. I was like, "Mom, we gotta get you some help, and fast!" I told her to call a stylist that she used to go to, *who knows what she is doing*, and I WOULD BE **HAPPY** TO PAY FOR IT!!!!

Well, the stylist was not feeling well, so she suggested that **I** (me – Carolyn Gray) shampoo and curl it, saying that should take care of it. Well I quickly reverted back to my Southern roots, and I was like, "Chile, please!" My mother's hair was uneven, damaged and dry – it didn't even look like she had a relaxer! What was I supposed to do? I have not been trained in cutting, styling and fixing chemical messes! Needless to say, we started asking around, and finally, I dropped her off at one of her favorite local stylists to get her some emergency conditioning treatments, a nice cut to even everything up and a set. However, when I picked her up, the lady had given her a Jheri Curl! Did I mention that my Mom lives in Georgia and she is 61? Anyway, in that area and age group, curls are still kinda popular. Even though I was a little shocked, it was actually very cute – all one length, a nice curly style for the summer, and Praise the Lord, she did not look like the Heat Mizer any more! She actually got a lot of compliments on her little curly do, and she did look cute for the wedding, just like she wanted! Yeah! So all's well that ends well, right?

Well maybe, *but maybe not*. This experience combined with my last few touch-up encounters has made me even more serious about protecting myself from potential foolishness with my future relaxers. I am beginning a brand new era of *Relaxing with Care*, which is why I have dedicated a chapter to it. I will not let years of hard work be ruined by poor quality perms, bad applications or a stylist's possible misuse of relaxers. The problems I have mentioned with my scalp and hair along with my mother's can be extremely frustrating, especially when you realize that they could have been easily avoided. I have to be honest, there have been times I have wanted to cry, especially with all the effort I have put into trying to have healthy hair. It's okay though, we all live and learn, and my eyes are now wide open. As a result, I am going to use some of the tips given in the next chapter to select a new stylist – I need someone closer so I will not mind going to the salon, and I also want to try a new relaxer. I don't think the brand I have used over the past few years has been good for my scalp or hair. I think it is time for me to try something different. I have heard some really good things about Affirm from a family member and people on the Internet. I think one of the most valuable lessons I have learned is that ***until you get the chemical part right, most of the other efforts you employ to keep your hair healthy may be in vain***. Over the years, I became complacent in this area (scared to make changes), but I encourage you not to make the same mistake. So, do relaxers require extra work and oversight? You better believe they do, and if you are not prepared for that, **relaxers may not be for you**, and more importantly, never put one in a child's hair until you are fully prepared to do all that is required to maintain it successfully.

If You Decide to Stick With Relaxers...

So I said all of the above to say that *we can have healthy, beautiful, relaxed hair,* but it takes extra work and care on our part. With that said, here are some steps we can all take to *relax with care*:

1. **Have your hair relaxed (or colored) by a licensed stylist whenever possible** *unless you are trained to do so* **and** *you feel really comfortable doing it.* It is hard enough for trained professionals to carefully apply relaxers to only new growth, neutralize and rinse all remaining traces of chemicals from your hair. However, it is almost impossible for someone to objectively look at all sections of their own head and to follow all of the required steps to *successfully* apply a relaxer without the risk of overlapping or overprocessing. Even if ill-results are not seen immediately (e.g., breakage, dryness, thinning, weak hair, etc.), that does not mean that you may not experience problems down the road. When picking a stylist to do this, be sure that you have seen some of their work first, namely their relaxed client's hair if possible.

2. **Do not confuse dry hair and new growth with being in need of a touch-up**. Try to go as far past the 8-week mark as you can in your relaxer where you don't experience excessive breakage (e.g., the point where you can't even comb the new growth, etc.). I understand that some women with shorter cuts may have a hard time hiding new growth, but relaxing every 6 weeks or less will eventually lead to damage. You may not see it for years (I didn't), but your hair or scalp will suffer in some way. I used to think I couldn't make it beyond the 5 or 6-week mark, but by regular shampooing (every 3-4 days) and moisturizing (I now use Healthier Hair in a Bottle! Oil Spray), I have been able to stretch my relaxers to 12 weeks and beyond, and my hair is healthier than it has been in years. Even if you can't go that long, try to wait a week longer each time until

you reach a comfortable point **past** the 6 week mark. Trying styles such as plait/braid/twist sets can help or putting your hair in a bun, updo (curl activator can help slick edges down) or braids/cornrows. However, *be sure to take your braids or cornrows down within two weeks of getting your touch-up to reduce the risk of scalp irritation.*

3. **Do not *ever* go to a relaxer or touch-up appointment with your hair and scalp feeling dry.** If your hair is not properly moisturized, the tendency for breakage or shedding in the bowl is greatly increased. Like a "big dummy" (*I keep thinking of this term from Sanford & Son as I look back at some of the things I have done*), I started going to my appointments with my hair and scalp all dried out. I used to be scared to shampoo less than 7 days before my touch-up, because of possible scalp irritation. *However, that was before I started doing cleansing rinses (using a conditioner instead of shampoo) or just shampooing the top layer of my hair without massaging the scalp.* Also, it never occurred to me to **ever** oil my scalp before getting this very drying and potentially irritating process done. Now at least a week before, I shampoo and **deep condition** (sit under a dryer or heating cap) my hair as described in one of the weeks from the Six-Week Regimen or do the Severely Dry Hair Treatment (described in Chapter 3) if my hair is drier than usual. I also do a Mid-Week/ Refresher shampoo (about 3 or 4 days before), but I don't massage the scalp. Afterwards, I usually let it dry with one plait/twist in the back or just let it dry straight in a pony-tail(s).

For the night before, I have found that putting a little Infusium 23 Leave-In Treatment (other leave-in treatments can work too) on the hair and ends provides some protection as well. I also massage a little Healthier Hair in a Bottle! Oil Spray into my scalp and on the hair too (again, other moisturizers can be used). However, in your moisturizing and pre-relaxer treatments ***make sure that your scalp does not get wet the night before or the day of*** – oil products are fine, but sweat, water and water-based liquids (e.g., leave-in treatments, Healthier Hair in a Bottle! Moisturizing & Detangling Mist, etc.) should be avoided. When the scalp is wet, or you are sweating, the skin becomes a lot more sensitive, especially the scalp, making it more prone to irritation. So it wouldn't be a good idea to go for a jog or do aerobics a few hours before getting a relaxer. However, if for some reason, you cannot avoid having a relaxer done after sweating, your stylist could minimize your risk of irritation by having you sit under a cool dryer to help close your pores.

4. **Speaking of your scalp... Make sure your scalp does not have any sores, cuts or irritated areas at the time a chemical is to be applied (e.g., relaxers, texturizers, color, etc.).** You would think stylists would check for this, but I don't think I have ever met one who has, so *you* need to check beforehand, and reschedule your appointment if necessary. You can help minimize the chance of this by not scratching your scalp with your fingernails or combs (you really shouldn't be doing this anyway) the week before. Also, try not to massage your scalp too vigorously – I often resort to patting my scalp to get rid of pesky itching, which my husband usually makes jokes about. I won't say it works totally, but it helps.

5. **Do not let a stylist apply permanent or semi-permanent color to your hair at the same appointment where your relaxer is being done.** *These types of appointments should be scheduled at least two weeks apart.* I don't care if the stylist says it is okay, and a number of them have told me that it is okay. As there are always exceptions, for some ladies having them done together may not be a problem, but what if you are not one of the lucky ones? What if you start seeing unexplainable patchiness or breakage? What if your scalp starts to burn more or be more sensitive than before? If you have scalp or hair problems that you don't have answers for, this could be a place to start. This was never an area I ever used to be concerned with until I hit my thirties, and I had my second child, then the gray hair started coming in full force (not just the usual 2 or 3 strands, but all around the front edges). Some people are okay with the gray, but for now, I have decided to fight it. As a result, I went from rinses to semi-permanent color, **and** because I don't like to go to the salon that often, **and** because my stylist said it was okay, **and** because I heard of other ladies who color and relax at

the same time, I decided to do it too. I have since come to regret this... I have had unexplainable scalp irritation and problems with breakage and thinning (after my chemical processes, not during the times before) – some might have been caused by overuse of relaxers, but others may have been related to doing too much (chemically) at once. Just food for thought... I have since given up on the semi-permanent coloring, and I now only cover the gray with a leave-in rinse (see Chapter 3) and a black touch-up wand, especially since new gray hairs start growing in almost immediately. So my new motto is, *the fewer heavy-duty chemicals, the better*. However, if you still use semi-permanent/permanent color, ***avoid doing the two processes at the same time.***

6. **Make sure that you/your stylist bases your hair and scalp thoroughly before relaxing.** I have experienced overprocessing and breakage in some areas where my edges were not based well. It seems like such a simple thing, but it can take weeks, months or years for some of us to recover. As we grow older, hair seems to fill in slower, especially around the edges, so this warning should be taken seriously just in case you are one of those women. This is an area where you definitely need to keep your eyes open. My problem is I stopped paying attention – a lot of times my hair appointments had turned into a social get together (catching up, listening to old school music) to the point that I did not think to check how well my stylist based my edges and scalp. When I visited her salon, she used to slather on a heavy base (e.g., petroleum jelly, or similar products) around my edges, but since she started coming to my house, as I think back, I can barely remember this step happening. Could that have been one of the reasons I started burning so quickly around my front edges or why there are now sensitive spots around my front edges? Who knows? There is so much room for error with relaxers that all we can do is pay attention, and realize that you and your stylist are a team. However, you definitely have more to lose, so don't try to put all of the responsibility *or blame* on them, and keep your eyes open, regardless who the stylist is or their credentials/reputation!

7. **Make sure that the relaxer is only applied to your new growth, not the hair that has already been relaxed.** I remember a stylist that I used to love back in the day told me that the next time I got my touch-up she was going to relax the full length of my hair because, "... *you need to straighten out the rest of the hair too*." Even though I didn't know any better at the time, this was the last time she ever saw me or did my hair! What was she thinking? I really don't know, but you can never assume that every stylist knows what they are doing, no matter how sincere or scientific they may sound! If you are able to, catch a glance in a mirror to make sure your stylist is only touching up the new growth, and even if you can't see, it won't hurt to *politely* confirm this with him/her in conversation. Overprocessing is a hard thing to recover from, so I wouldn't worry about offending someone, especially as much as we pay to get these chemicals put in!

8. **Also, don't get caught up in trying to get your hair relaxed bone straight each time – I mean to the point where there is little elasticity or life left in your hair.** Some of us are pretty obsessed with having our hair as straight as it can be, which is why we often leave relaxers on too long and invest in blow dryers and flat irons that are too hot and paddle brushes that are too hard. Our hair needs to have some elasticity (*the ability to stretch or be pulled without popping immediately*) left in it. Otherwise, the hair is weak and very prone to excessive breakage. Some curl left is a good thing – *we are Black, aren't we?*

9. **Make sure that you/your stylist neutralizes, shampoos and rinses thoroughly after your relaxer.** If any of these areas are neglected, the caustic chemicals in your relaxer can continue to break down your hair **long** after your appointment is over. This is how some people's hair breaks off as it is being combed days and weeks after an appointment. Scary, but true. Then when you go back to confront a stylist, some may say, "Oh, maybe it is a medication you are taking." In rare cases maybe, but in most, the relaxer was not applied or removed properly. This is one of the main reasons I suggest a professional stylist is consulted for the application of chemicals, but even with them, you still have to keep your eyes open! However, if you do relax your own hair, I don't think rinsing in your kitchen sink provides the necessary water pressure to thoroughly

rinse strong chemicals from your hair. I noticed that I experienced a little breakage in all of the hard to rinse areas (e.g., side edges and back edges behind my ears) once I started having my stylist come to my house, doing my hair in the kitchen and rinsing in the kitchen sink. To make matters worse, she is shorter than I am, so I know she struggled to reach certain areas. We even tried doing a final rinse in my bathtub to get more pressure, but I think having this process done in a salon, where you are lying back in a chair, and the stylist can see all angles of your head works best. I think this can eliminate a lot of the risk of leaving trace amounts of the relaxer in your hair. If you have any questions or doubts about how thoroughly you have been shampooed or rinsed, **speak up immediately** (don't wait until afterwards) – *remember my mother's experience?* After the final rinse, I think it is also extremely important that a deep conditioning treatment is done – some stylists may try to bypass this, but you should make sure that they not only apply a conditioner, but also have you **sit under a dryer with it as well**. This is something you should talk to them about before scheduling the appointment because it is a pain to argue with someone about this while your hair is soaking wet. Believe me, I have had to do it – more than once too! This may seem like a little thing yes, but it is definitely worth the effort.

10. **Don't let your guard down just because a stylist says they are using a no-lye, "kiddie" or "mild" perm on your hair.** Regardless of the title placed next to the word "relaxer" or the manufacturer's claims, *all relaxers are caustic and dangerous*, requiring equal care before, during and after their application. All tips mentioned above still apply, regardless of the type of relaxer you are using. I don't care what the stylist says. This is one of the main reasons I would encourage parents to wait as long as you can before relaxing a young girl's hair because many children and adults have had their hair messed up with so-called "kiddie" or "no-lye" perms. So regardless of the name, you still have to be careful. I hate to sound like a pessimist, but there just does not to seem to be any fool-proof or easy answer when it comes to relaxing, which is why this chapter is called, *Relaxing with Care* – which I think is the best we can do, aside from *staying natural*.

If you are reading this, and your hair is natural and you *were* contemplating getting a relaxer, you might now be scared to go through with it. Believe me, I am not trying to scare anyone, as you already know I have a relaxer myself! With that said though, I can speak from **experience**, not just research, when I say that **relaxers are no joke, and they are not for everyone!** So *before you put one in your hair or your child's hair, you should think long and hard*, and make sure you are ready to do what is required. If you are not, maybe you should think some more before going forward with it. Pressing/straightening can be a safer, healthier option to consider until you are totally sure. Dermatologists are starting to warn that *we* are doing grave, long-term damage to our hair and scalp by the overuse/misuse of these dangerous chemicals. So until you are sure that you are ready to relax with care, I say *sisters beware*!

Chapter 8

Selecting A Stylist

Although I believe that 90% of the responsibility for the general condition and appearance of our hair is up to us, I do believe that a good stylist is worth their weight in gold! If you apply any type of chemical (e.g., relaxer, texturizer, color, curls, etc.) to your hair or press/straighten it, a good stylist is ***invaluable***. So many of our hair troubles start with the misuse or abuse of chemicals that any stylist who can use them skillfully **and** help keep our hair healthy should be considered a blessing from above. Even with the importance of selecting the right person to take care of our hair, most people spend more time picking out a breakfast cereal than they do a stylist! Because the stylist you choose is, *hopefully*, going to help you reach your short-term and long-term hair goals, you should select one with great prayer and consideration.

As you search for the right stylist for you, don't assume that someone is good because their services are expensive or they operate in an upscale salon. You never know, the best stylist for you may own or work in a very small, *no-frills* salon. A stylist's talent, skill and ability to help us has nothing to do with the glamour or trendiness of their salon or its location, their clientele list (*I am not impressed by celebrity customers*), or the hair shows they have attended. ***All I care about is can you do some hair?*** Do you care enough to do your best work and give your customers their money's worth? Can you be trusted to make good decisions based on the client's current hair situation, history and their best interest (e.g., not giving someone a relaxer and color job when you see that there is not significant new growth and the scalp is already irritated from previous chemical treatments)? Is it too much to just want a stylist who will have our back, who will recommend attractive, healthy styles and chemicals that are suited to our hair needs? As with everything else, we have to keep our eyes open, and do our homework before trusting one of our most prized possessions to a relative stranger. We can't really take a lot for granted either. As an example, just because a stylist can work the heck out of some weaves and extensions does not mean that they are the best person to press/straighten your hair or the best one to color or relax your hair!

There are so many factors to consider – the current condition of your hair, what you want done, and the level of information and maintenance support you need. I would start off by asking ladies with *healthy-looking* hair where they go to get their hair done. You can also find helpful resources on the Internet (e.g., black hair groups, salon listings, etc.). Ask around, and check a few out. No one can really make the selection for you, but here are some tips to hopefully make your selection a little easier:

1. Select a *currently* licensed professional, not someone who *used to be* or *will be* licensed.

2. Select someone that is neat, clean and professional in appearance. Also, check the condition of the person's hair to see how they treat their *best customer*.

3. Select a stylist who has a neat, clean and professional work environment. They should have modern hair appliances and utensils that are clean and in good working order.

4. Select someone that you feel comfortable with – someone that you feel you can trust and talk to candidly about what you like and don't like (**very important**). Also, make sure they respect your wishes and feelings.

5. Select a hair professional who uses products you are familiar with (e.g., relaxers, color, etc.). Always ask what their products of choice are and *why*, especially for relaxers.

6. Talk to at least two customer references (or at least one **really good one**, if you can't get two) that the prospective stylist has performed chemical procedures on as well as hair trimming or cutting before making your final decision.

7. To help you make your final decision, allow a stylist that has made it through the criteria specified above, to perform a simple service on your hair like a shampoo and set. As they are doing your hair make sure you talk to get their opinion on your hair, its condition and their recommendations on how you should treat or style it in the future. It is pretty hard for anyone to mess up a shampoo and set, but this experience will allow you to determine if your earlier assessment of the prospective stylist is correct. If it is, you have done your best to find the right stylist for you.

If you have followed at least a few of the tips that apply to you (*I know no one will do all of them*), you have hopefully found someone pretty decent, even if you had a to go through a couple of *bad apples* in the process. There are just no guarantees – *stylists are human too*. However, being the paranoid person I am, I say that even after you find someone, you should still:

1. **Trust your instincts** when it comes to decisions about your hair. The stylist may be the professional, but it is your head! *You* pay the stylist, so *your opinion matters*. *You* have the final say in what happens to your hair!

2. **Monitor your own hair history**. Never let a stylist relax your hair more than once every six weeks. Instead, ask them to give you suggestions or styles that can help you stretch your relaxer out longer for the overall health of your hair and scalp. Also, remember the name of the chemical(s) used on your hair, and *question changes*.

3. If you are getting a relaxer or any chemical treatment for the first time (e.g., permanent color, texturizer, body wave, etc.) **make sure your stylist does a strand test** to determine the correct relaxer strength or appropriate product to use, especially if you are not familiar with his/her work.

4. **Never allow a stylist to put relaxer on your ends during a touch-up.** I think we should sometimes work on being quiet during the application of a relaxer because too many times we are talking to the stylist (this is the case for me), which can distract them from their task and cause us, *and them,* not to pay attention. In case no one has ever said it to you, *we all should be paying attention during chemical treatments.*

5. Always request to **sit under the dryer or a heating cap with a conditioner** and/or a reconstructor after a relaxer or touch-up.

6. Until trust has been established (*and even after*), **always** look in a mirror or monitor the floor when having your hair trimmed or cut. If not, get the stylist to *show* you how much they plan to take off *first*.

7. Also, until trust is established *always ask questions* (politely and respectfully, of course), especially during chemical procedures (e.g., So you are applying the neutralizer now? – I actually said this at a Hair Cuttery once, and I felt it *really* needed to be asked). While you are keeping your eyes open and asking questions, make sure all chemicals are rinsed out thoroughly. If you have any doubts ask if they can do *one last rinse,* even if you have to say something like, "I think I still feel something on my scalp..." This is a whole lot better than kicking yourself for months afterwards if it wasn't rinsed thoroughly and you experience breakage or other problems!

8. Space relaxer and coloring (permanent or semi-permanent) appointments *at least* 2 weeks apart – **do *not* relax and color at the same time.** Even if the stylist or the product label says it is okay, having done them together before, *I would wait* – **it is better to be safe than sorry.**

9. If you visit a salon regularly, **do not allow your stylist to blow dry your hair more than once every six weeks.** I say this because I have visited salons where they only wanted to blow dry and hot curl my relaxed hair, and stylists have tried to convince me that it was okay. However, the results that I got during those periods quickly helped me to see that *it was not.*

10. **Never allow *anyone* to abuse your hair**! This means do not allow your stylist to run a comb through your hair from the roots to the ends unless your hair has been detangled first. Also, never let your stylist brush your hair wet. You are responsible for your hair, so you have to speak up!

11. **Re-evaluate your stylist selection as needed**, especially if the stylist starts sentences with the word "Look" when you voice your concerns or opinions about your hair. As an example, "Look, I don't have time to..." or "Look, I can't be..." If the use of these types of phrases makes you think that a stylist doesn't care about your feelings or desires where your hair is concerned, you may still need to "*look*" for another stylist. I have experienced this before where a stylist basically did not feel like taking the time to style my hair the way I wanted him to. He even had the nerve to argue with me and tell me, "Look, your hair is too long (it was shoulder length) for it to be full on the top." In other words, it was late, he was tired, and he did not feel like doing a spiral curl on my hair even though I told him I was going to be in a wedding and I needed a style that would last in the summer heat. I know I must have spent at least 4 or 5 hours there, but instead of spiral curls, he blow dried my hair and bumped the ends, and he charged me over $100 (a touch-up, trim and style in a "supposed" to be upscale salon in Washington, D.C.)! Needless to say, he did not get a tip, and he never saw me or my money again. The moral of the story: You are paying, so don't tolerate blatant disrespect – no one is that good!

12. Finally, and most importantly, when you find the right stylist for you, stick with them. **Do Not Chair Hop!** Find one good person, and only switch when absolutely necessary. Once your stylist learns about you, your hair, chemical history and goals for your hair, that person can be one of the best allies you can have in your

quest for healthier, beautiful hair. They may not be as prone to make careless mistakes that can cost you years of progress. One can only hope, but still *keep your eyes open*.

Hopefully I didn't go overboard on the tips, but I just don't want anyone to make mistakes like I have made. It is not like we are deciding the fate of the world, but letting a stranger loose on our hair with chemicals, scissors or a hot comb can be a scary process. *I know it is for me.* Regardless, *having a stylist we trust and like is a such a blessing*, so you really should try to find one. However, even after you do, as I have said before, you still have to *keep your eyes open*, making sure that your hair is being well taken care of and that your stylist is helping you in your quest for healthier hair, not taking you off course.

CHAPTER 9

GROWING LONGER HAIR & KEEPING IT!

… if a woman have long hair, it is a glory to her.

I Corinthians 11:15 (*New King James Version*)

*However, even if she doesn't have it or doesn't want it, we all know that **she is still beautiful and glorious!** This chapter is for those of us who want longer hair – **just because we want it!** No other reason is needed, "we just want it!" If you have no interest in growing longer hair, please move on to Chapter 10.*

I would like to re-affirm my belief that there is no "good" or "bad" hair – **we all have good hair**! *We just sometimes have bad hair care habits or regimens, which is something that we can definitely correct.* As a result, I believe if we want longer, healthier hair, **we *can* grow it ourselves**. I think in most cases, the information given in this book so far can help us do that. I still have a strong desire to prove that black women can grow long, healthy hair (*part of my ministry thing again, bear with me!*) – weaves, extensions and wigs are not the only way for us to have long hair! **We *can* grow hair, our ends *can* be healthy, and we *can* keep up with the latest styles at the same time**! It is my hope that this book will empower us to do all of these things! Now with that said…

Our Hair Does Grow!

Hair grows an average of ½ inch per month for a woman whose body and scalp are relatively healthy. However, for some fortunate women it could grow as much as ¾ of an inch, depending on heredity, diet and overall health. So, even when it doesn't seem like your hair is growing, it is actually growing almost an inch every two months, on average. So, every year, you could possibly grow up to six new inches of hair! However, if you do not care for your hair properly, you could lose that much in split-ends or breakage alone. If this happens, at the end of the year, it would look as if your hair did not grow at all, when actually it grew a lot. *You just did not retain the length.* Funny enough, this can also happen when you allow *excessive* trimming to occur, but we'll talk more about that later.

My Personal Whine Fest!

When I look around and I see the countless numbers of women of other ethnic backgrounds (e.g., Caucasions, Latinos, Middle Easterners, Indians, Chinese, etc.) with long flowing hair that *seems* to grow so easily, I have sometimes said, "God this ain't hardly fair!" In fact, when I get to heaven, I plan to ask the Lord why it *seems* that we are the only ones that struggle to grow and keep hair! Why is it that an Indian girl can keep her hair loose and flowing, season in and season out, and it will continue to grow like a weed? However, if the average sister who is trying to grow hair does this, she will see more breakage or damaged ends than she can sweep up or have trimmed off, losing the little length she might have acquired over the years. God knows my heart, so I can openly say that I think this is *really, really* unfair. I say this because, sometimes it does not feel like growing hair is an equal opportunity event. We all should be able to grow hair with ease, but I often wonder why must it be so hard for us? I think this is why there is a *rarely spoken* myth that sisters are not able to grow hair. This myth is further perpetuated by the fact that you see so many of us wearing wigs, weaves and extensions on a regular basis, not just for special occasions. It is has gotten so bad that even when *we* see a sister with long hair, some of us will look at her and skeptically say, "That ain't hardly her hair!" Believe me I have heard women say this. Even *we* sometimes act like we can't grow hair. Although we know this myth is ***not*** true, the average sister cannot deny that it does take a lot of work and patience for us to get really long hair, especially when chemicals are involved. Believe me I know!

One of the reasons I think this is so unfair is because you can have two women with the same facial features and body type – one has hair down her back while the other has short/medium hair. In too many cases, our society often views the woman with long hair as most attractive. Although we may not agree with this, too many of us have seen how crazy some brothers go when they see a girl who may not be all that attractive, but she is skinny and flinging some hair around, even if it is not real! Does this really matter, should we really care? The answer is obviously "no", but some of us may admit to being annoyed by these attitudes at various times in our lives, especially during our younger years. I remember being envious during the Prince and Purple Rain Era, where you had people like Vanity and Appolonia swinging hair for days, and I have to admit that *I wanted me some hair too*, especially when I saw the way guys my age were going crazy over them! I also remember seeing Robin Givens in Boomerang – they had her hair looking too good! I don't know if she had a weave or extensions, but after that movie, I wanted my hair to look like that, and I didn't care whether I grew it or bought it! Unfortunately, my husband fought against me buying it, although he did make an exception with a long pony-tail I wore after a bad trimming experience. Sometimes you just want more hair than you have, and you wish there was an easier way to get it, and you look at other women and wonder how is it that their hair grows so fast – I know I am not by myself in this.

Still Whining, But Moving On…

As we get older, it becomes more a matter of **what we want for ourselves**, *not what others like or what they think we should have.* For many women, long hair helps them appear and feel more glamorous, more youthful and often makes a woman with strong features look softer, more feminine. I don't think I have ever "hated" on women with long, beautiful hair, but as I observed some of the *perks* that can come with having hair, I decided that if we want longer hair "we" should be able to grow it too! And not just by buying it either, *doggone it, which is what too many of us have resorted to!* Okay, so now I have whined enough about how unfair I think it is that we seem to have to work so much harder than other groups to grow longer hair. However, as with anything in life, we have to make the best of the cards we are dealt and work toward a solution. *And* this my dear sisters is what I have spent the last few years trying to do, with renewed conviction, for myself, and for those of you reading this book.

This chapter is almost therapy for me as I rant and whine about this whole "hair growing" thing to someone other than my husband! I had these feelings of unfairness back in the 20th century, and I still have these feelings today, in the 21st century! It just bothers me when I see the efforts a lot of us have to go to get really long hair. As an example, I ran across a group of women on the Internet who experience great results (some have hair close to waist-length), but they wear their hair in protective styles (e.g., buns covered by drawstring pony-tails, braids or use hair pieces) most of the time. I also remember a black model, whose hair I always admired, that recommended keeping the hair pinned up most of the time in order to acquire serious length. When I see and hear this, I still find myself bugging God with the question, "Why we gotta work so hard to keep our length?" For a brief moment, I considered going to these lengths to get my hair to the next level in hair growth (I'm talking past the bra strap now, maybe even waist length!), and I even wore my hair in a bun for about a week straight. The bun was cute, don't get me wrong, but I don't like to be limited in how I can wear my hair, and I surely don't want to wear hair pieces for long periods of time to *protect* my hair. *This defeats the whole purpose for me.*

I want to grow longer hair, **but I want to be able to wear my hair however I want to, whenever I want to,** *using some common sense of course.* I see White, Latin, Asian and Middle-Eastern women wearing their hair down, flinging it all winter long, but many would have us believe that we have to keep ours pinned up if we want to acquire serious length. I will admit that many of them don't use the strong chemicals we use on our hair, and they usually shampoo more frequently. Even so, after thinking about it long and hard, I decided that this whole ideology is **not** acceptable to me. *I am not knocking or discounting the methods of ladies who find success doing* *this in anyway, especially since I have seen some of the results, but I just know it is not for me.* So this chapter is mainly devoted to sharing ideas that I have about what we can do to grow longer, healthier hair while we go about our normal lives, *wearing our normal styles.* I think this is important, especially for ladies whose hair may be too short to even get it into a *protective* style, and what is the fun of having hair if you can't wear it how you want?

Breaking Barriers

Many of us attribute our inability to grow hair past a certain length to heredity, but for the most part, the length of our hair is determined by how well we care for it. I remember telling one of my sisters-in-law that I wanted to grow my hair long like one of my cousin's whose hair was well past her shoulders, and she shared her belief that it is in your genes – *either you can grow hair, or you can't!* Looking around, I had to admit that most of my cousins and family members, mainly on my mom's side, had relatively short hair, and my mother has never even had shoulder-length hair as far as I know. So I was almost tempted to agree with my sister-in-law, especially after years of struggling to get my hair past my shoulders. I actually have to thank my sister-in-law for this because I like to prove people wrong when they are skeptical about something I want to do, and when she said, *"Either you can grow hair, or you can't."* I became determined to prove her wrong. In fact, reaching my goal (at the time, I just wanted my hair to touch my shoulder blades, *like my sister-in-law's daughter*) is how I came to write the first edition of this book. I had just put together a regimen for myself that helped me finally grow my hair past my shoulders, without split-ends, and without me being pregnant. So with the first book I was very excited, and with it being my first book, I did not really have any experience *keeping* the length that I acquired, so looking back I realize that there was a lot more for me to learn and to say. Now, a few years later, I can honestly say *I have been through a few things, had a few trials and tribulations* where my hair is concerned, and I now have some experience fighting the good fight where keeping my length is concerned! As a result, **all** of the chapters of this book have been overhauled and updated (i.e., *Six-Week Regimen, Daily Hair Care, etc.)* with new and improved tips and methods designed to not only help us grow hair, but also to ***keep it***. With that said, here are a few suggestions, in addition to the previous chapters, that might help:

1. Remember that **no hair care product can "cause" or guarantee hair growth!** Some products may facilitate hair growth or minimize breakage and split-ends so that growth is more noticeable, but hair growth is not caused by the use of external products. *So there is no easy answer to growing longer hair.*

2. If you truly want longer hair, **you are going to have to take control**. *You can't put the responsibility of your hair's condition or length on your stylist.* It really isn't their job or responsibility. The job of a stylist is mainly to cut, style and apply chemicals to your hair. In fact, many of them have not been trained how to care for hair on a daily basis (e.g., what to do, which products and how they should be used, etc.) or how to treat hair for maximum growth. As a result, you must realize that just because a person is a licensed stylist and can make your hair look good in the salon, it does not mean that they can necessarily help us grow longer hair. So you still have to keep your eyes open, especially for chemical services, and make sure you do your part!

It took me almost two years to realize that my hair often received more abuse at the hands of a "professional" stylist than it did when I was at home. Have you ever noticed how rough some stylists are with our hair? Roughly or quickly pulling the comb through it, blow drying it and using a hot curler to style it even though we may have weak or damaged hair, not making us sit under the dryer with a deep conditioner after a touch-up. Some of this happens because of a lack of knowledge or experience on their parts, but many times it is a result us sitting there quietly, not complaining about it. So as we are going for our hair appointments (e.g., chemical treatments, trims, etc.), we have to speak up more when there is a problem, and we can't be afraid to find someone new. Check out Chapter 8 for more tips on this.

3. For those of you who really want longer hair, it is critical that you **keep your hair clean, well-conditioned, protected from heat styling and carefully handled**. You need to be especially diligent about following the regimen found in this book (or a similar regimen), especially the tips found in Chapters 3, 4, 5 and 6 (the Six-Week Regimen, Drying Methods, Daily Hair Care and Styling chapters). Your key to success is *commitment* and *consistency* – you must be committed to growing longer hair, and you must be willing to consistently take care of it.

4. **Pay attention to your diet.** Contrary to what we often read hair growth is stimulated and nourished by the blood circulation underneath the scalp – *not by products*. Because of this, you must be concerned not only with what happens to the outside surface of your hair, but also what goes into your body. For overall health and the health of our hair, drink plenty of water (at least eight glasses a day, which may help get us slimmer as a bonus), eat right (e.g., fruits, vegetables, low-fat calcium-rich and protein-rich foods, etc.), get regular exercise, and *some form* of a multi-vitamin supplement. These basic steps will ensure that your scalp and hair have a healthy internal foundation to start the ball rolling.

Did you notice that I said *some form* of a multi-vitamin supplement? I say this because some women can get away with just taking a One-a-Day or Geritol vitamin supplement, and they are totally healthy, and they can reach their hair care goals with relative ease. However, there are some women *like me,* who because of diet, heredity, medications, nutritional deficiencies, or whatever have to go a little above and beyond to get the same results. Again, all things don't seem fair, but it is okay because there are products on the market that can supplement our diets and vitamin regimen, if we feel we need something above and beyond.

Vitamins Above & Beyond

As I endured challenge after challenge to get my hair to reach my bra strap while it's straight (e.g., overprocessing, too many chemicals, bad trims, absentmindedly forgetting to moisturize, etc.), I started wondering what I could do to improve the texture, strength and growth rate of my *new* hair. I had heard of other women who were taking large doses of vitamins and were claiming to have increased the rate that their hair grew. I have to admit that I was, and still am, skeptical, but I already tried growing hair without supplements and experienced some pretty decent results, but I wondered what would happen if I added some of the supposedly hair-friendly ones to my diet. I do know that we can definitely improve the look and feel of our hair, skin and nails with improved nutrition, and vitamin and mineral supplements are a part of that, so I decided to try at least one.

I started off with GNC's Ultra Nourishair vitamin, but I decided to still research some of the vitamins and minerals I heard a number of women raving about. I ran across a couple of books at the library: The Real Vitamin & Mineral Book Using Supplements for Optimum Health Second Edition by Shari Lieberman & Nancy Bruning; and Vitamins for Dummies by Christopher Hobbs & Elson Haas. These books contain some pretty interesting vitamin information, *not just for hair care but for overall health as well,* and the next thing you know I was at my annual ob/gyn appointment with a gift bag full of vitamin and mineral supplements for the doctor to approve. After getting the green light, I developed a vitamin "habit", and now my kitchen cabinet is full of bottles from Evening Primrose to Silica! Some of you may just want to stop with the generic multi-vitamin or "hair" vitamin, which may work great for you (*I did get results before consistently taking any vitamins and even more with just the GNC hair vitamin*). However, if you are interested in going above and beyond or getting more information to help you make a better selection, you may want to check out some of the information below. Some of it, I have *heard* over the years, but most was pulled from the two previously mentioned sources.

NOTE: The recommended doses mentioned below are based on the sources I found and are **only for adults**, not for anyone under the age of 18. Also, as I did, **check with your personal physician before taking any type of vitamin or mineral supplement**. A trusted pediatrician or general family practicioner should also be consulted regarding vitamin supplements for children and early teens.

Riboflavin (Vitamin B2)

This vitamin facilitates the production of energy from foods and supports healthy skin, hair and nails. It is helpful in treating stress and fatigue and is especially beneficial for women who are taking estrogen products related to birth control or menopause.

- Small amounts of it are found in grains, fruits and vegetables. More may be found in brewer's yeast, liver, and oily fish such as salmon.
- Many experts believe that the average person only needs about 2 mg a day. However, many B-complex supplements contain 50-100 mg.
- There is no known toxicity related to riboflavin.

Pantothenic Acid (Vitamin B5)

It is often known as the "anti-stress" vitamin. Taken along with vitamin C, this vitamin can help strengthen hair and skin. Some researchers think that sufficient supplies of this can stop or limit hair from *graying (so far this has not been the case for me)*.

- The best sources are eggs, potatoes, saltwater fish, whole grain cereal and fresh vegetables such as sweet potatoes, green peas, cauliflower and avocados. However much of it is lost from foods when they are canned, cooked, frozen or processed.
- The recommended daily amount is around 10 mg daily. However, it is commonly taken at 100 to 500 mg daily.
- There is no known toxicity related to doses beyond this, but when a person experiences a deficiency they may experience premature graying of the hair.

Pyridoxine (Vitamin B6)

This vitamin helps the body use protein to build tissue, boost the metabolism of fats and produce red blood cells. It is also helpful in alleviating PMS symptoms. A deficiency of B6 can result in anemia. If you are on a high-protein diet, your body may require more B6.

- Only small amounts are found in whole foods. However, more can be found in wheat and organ meats like liver.

- *Consistently taking large doses could result in neurological damage* (often found in people taking more than 2,000 mg a day). However, dependencies have occurred in normal adults who took 200 mg a day for 30 days. This dependency results in a deficiency when the dosage is stopped abruptly.
- Some reports indicate that oral contraceptives can deplete vitamin B6 reserves, and it is recommended that at least 50 mg be taken a day to offset some of the symptoms often associated with this method of birth control (e.g., lethargy, fatigue, depression, etc.).

Biotin (Vitamin B7)

Along with vitamins A, B2 and B6, this vitamin is known to heal eczema and prevent hair loss, as well as strengthen nails and hair. Some have even said that it helps keep hair from graying (*again, I have not seen this yet, but one can only hope*).

- Biotin can be found in foods such as rice, chicken, egg yolks, brewer's yeast, soybeans, milk, cheese, saltwater fish and whole wheat flour.
- For optimum good health, some recommend that 150-300 mcg be taken daily.
- Biotin is considered to be non-toxic in doses beyond the recommended daily amount, and deficiencies are rare.

Vitamin E

Aside from the benefits of this vitamin to the hair, skin and nails, it is a great vitamin for women in general. It is said to help prevent certain cancers such as those affecting the cervix, lungs, gastrointestinal tract and possibly those related to the breasts. It is also known to help lessen the symptoms of fibrocystic breast disease. In fact, my ob/gyn recommended that I take vitamin E to relieve symptoms from this disease, but I didn't start taking it consistently until I heard about the potential benefits for my hair and skin. *It is a shame to be so vain!*

- The daily recommended 30 IUs can be safely increased to at least 400 IUs according to some experts. However, it is said that more than this could cause sores around the mouth, diarrhea and gastric upset. Is this true? I don't know, but why take any chances? I say let's just stick with doses of 400 IUs and below *unless your doctor recommends more.*

Zinc

Zinc is an essential component within our body, and the highest concentrations of it are found in areas such as our hair, eyes, bones, etc. Zinc is also known to prevent the absorption of lead, which we are exposed to through our drinking water and automobile fumes. It is also said to help protect us from substances that contribute to cancer and other disorders, as well as helping our bodies fight free radicals. It has also been recommended for the treatment of temporary hair loss.

- It is found in foods such as wheat germ, oysters and peas.
- Some experts recommend that men and women take between 22.5-50 mg a day for optimal health. However, you should not take more than 50 mg a day. An overdose can eventually lower the levels of HDL (the good cholesterol in your body), and some studies indicate that it could also cause serious illnesses such as cancer. Taking more than 100 mg a day could contribute to a heart attack. Is this true? I don't know, but this is why *it is very important to check with your personal physician **before** taking supplements to make sure there are not hidden risks given your medical history.*

Iron

Iron – *the menstruating woman's friend*. This is an element that we can usually get enough of from eating a balanced diet that is rich in leafy greens, lean red meat and whole-grain cereals and by popping an over-the-counter multi-vitamin supplement like One-a-Day or Geritol. However, if your diet is not so balanced (I'd have to raise my hand now), and/or you have heavy periods, you could periodically suffer from iron deficiencies. Some of the symptoms are fatigue, shortness of breath, heart palpitations (*this happened to me*), feeling unusually cold, desires to eat ice and some even have cravings to eat chalk (I had this happen in college during a chemistry class, and I thought I was going crazy). Sometimes the effects can also be seen in your hair (e.g., excessive shedding, thinning, dryness, etc.). Although every woman is different, ***it is best that you have a physician check your hemoglobin*** before trying to self-diagnose yourself for this condition. After suffering from anemia on and off for the past 20 years, my internist (after ruling out fibroids) said I am someone who should probably always take an iron supplement, which is why I take one along with my hair vitamin. **If your doctor determines that you need one**, read the following warnings:

- Iron is a very dangerous supplement to take around children. I have heard that iron overdoses are one of the most common ways that children under 6 are accidentally and **fatally** poisoned. So if you ever drop one anywhere kids are, *it is critical you find it.* While on the subject of iron, ***only give it to kids or teens if their physician recommends it.***
- Taking more than 18 mg (the minimum daily requirement for most women, but 30 mg for pregnant women) of iron has been found to increase the risk of heart attack, infections and certain types of cancer. *A good rule is not to take any extra iron without consulting with your doctor first.* Once absorbed, iron is not excreted from the body, which is why too much in the form of supplements can build up and cause problems.
- Vitamin C helps your body absorb iron, so drinking a glass of orange juice (or other drink containing it) with it may be helpful.

Silicon (Silica)

This is one of the most commonly found elements in the earth's soil and in foods. It supports and strengthens your skin, hair and nails.

- Naturally occurs in plant fibers, whole grains, and in vegetables such as beets, lettuce, cucumbers and onions.
- There is no recommended daily intake, but sources indicate that you may take up to 50 mg or more daily.
- Other sources indicate that too much silicon, above 50 mg a day, could lead to Alzheimer's disease. Is this true? Again, I have no idea, but **check with your doctor before taking this or any other supplement.**

Inositol

This is a *vitamin-like* substance that is found in soy lecithin along with choline. It helps the body to metabolize fat and supports healthy hair and skin. From many accounts, your body can create all of the inositol it needs, so it appears unnecessary to get this substance from our daily diet. However, most "hair" vitamins contain inositol.

- It is found in whole grains, molasses, wheat germ and nuts.
- There are no known requirements for this substance.

- There are no concerns regarding toxicity or deficiency. However, if there is a deficiency, it might appear in your hair and skin.

MSM (Methylsulfonylmethane)

MSM is an organic source of sulfur. Sulfur is an important part of a number of amino acids, and it helps the body to synthesize protein. It is also a critical component in the formation of collagen, connective tissue and cartilage – items necessary for healthy skin, hair, and joints. It is also a component in various enzymes that help the body eliminate and deactivate many kinds of toxins in our bodies.

- Primarily found in protein-rich foods such as eggs, dairy products, meat and fish. Also found in vegetables such as cabbage, turnips, onions, garlic and some beans.
- There is no recommended daily amount, but many experts suggest doses of 500-1,000 mg a day.
- There is no known toxicity or deficiencies associated with this substance.

Evening Primrose Oil

This oil is extracted from the evening primrose plant, and it contains omega-6 fatty acids (gamma-linolenic acids) that your body uses to lubricate skin and tissues and enables cell membranes to function normally. These fatty acids are essential for healthy skin and hair. They have been known to improve conditions such as dry skin and hair, dandruff and hair loss. They also help with conditions such as fibrocystic breast disease (my ob/gyn recommended it), PMS symptoms and skin conditions such as eczema and psoriasis.

- Some sources recommend a daily dosage of 2,000-3,000 mg.
- There are no known levels of toxicity.

Flaxseed Oil

This is probably one of the most balanced and nutritious oils because it contains both omega-3 and omega-6 fatty acids. It is used to treat some of the same symptoms as Evening Primrose Oil (described above). Many believe that flaxseed oil is a cancer and cardio-protector, as well as an estrogen regulator. For this reason, some breast cancer patients include flaxseed, as an oil or powder, in their diets.

- The recommended dosage is two-four teaspoons or up to five or six capsules.
- There are no known levels of toxicity.

• ~ • ~ • ~~ • ~ • ~ •

IMPORTANT NOTE: Although the vitamins/minerals listed above boast many health benefits, and some people may have success with them, those of you new to a vitamin regimen, should be aware that results may not be seen for weeks or months. Also, to manage expectations, I think it should be said that the results of consistent vitamin use will only affect the new hair that grows – so *your enhanced nutrition and its benefits will mainly be seen in the new hair that is growing from your scalp.* I say this so that you won't be disappointed if you don't see a big difference in the hair you already have.

After giving this information, again I say, **please consult your physician before taking any kind of supplement, especially if you are pregnant, nursing, on medication, or if you have any medical or psychiatric condition.** After doing so, if you decide to take a supplement(s) try the following tips to maximize your body's absorption of these vitamins and minerals:

- For the most part, vitamins work best when taken as a part of a balanced formula, so keep this in mind when selecting supplements. This is especially relevant with B vitamins (e.g., B1, B2, B6, etc.) which should be taken as a formula combination for the most part, not individually. Supplement formulas usually combine the appropriate combination of vitamins/nutrients, and for them to work as intended, they should be ingested in a proper balance.
- Take supplements with meals (up to 10 minutes before or up to 30 minutes after a meal).
- Increase or decrease your doses gradually – don't jump from a very small dose to a very large dose.
- Buy natural supplements that don't contain coal tars, artificial coloring, preservatives, and other additives such as sugar.
- Store your supplements in a cool, dark, dry place and be sure to check expiration dates.
- Remember that potential deficiencies exist for vegetarians for protein, iron, zinc, calcium and B-12. So if you are a vegetarian, in addition to supplements, you should make sure your diet contains a good amount of low-fat dairy products, nuts, seeds, green leafy vegetables and beans.
- Finally, **be consistent! Take your vitamins daily – Make it about your health, not just about your hair!**

Okay now that I shared all of this generic vitamin information, I am sure you are wondering what I am taking. Well, I can't say I have a "perfect" or "guaranteed" vitamin regimen for you – I wish I could, but I can't. However, I am starting to see benefits from the little routine I made up. For those of you who are interested, I will share the actual names of the products I am using (*like always*) along with the dosages. As with the hair care products I mentioned earlier, **I am just sharing,** *I am not saying that anyone should use the same products I do.* However, if you decide to adopt a similar routine, please be sure to get your doctor's approval **before** starting. I cannot say this enough, and it could be as simple as a phone call. Everybody is different – *just because something works for me, does not mean that it is okay for you!* So with all that said, every morning after breakfast I take the following supplements with a glass of calcium-enriched orange juice:

- **1 GNC UltraNourish Hair Vitamin** tablet (*the serving size is really 2 tablets, but I only take one because I am cheap, and I take other supplements*), which contains the following:

		% Daily Value
Vitamin A (100% as beta-Carotene)	500 IU	10%
Vitamin C (as Ascorbic Acid)	30 mg	50%
Vitamin E (as natural d-alpha Tocopheryl Succinate)	15 IU	50%
Thiamin (Vitamin B-1) (as Thiamin Mononitrate)	.75 mg	50%
Riboflavin (Vitamin B-2)	.85 mg	50%
Niacin (as Niacinamide)	10 mg	50%
Vitamin B-6 (as Pyridoxine Hydrochloride)	2 mg	100%
Folic Acid	100 mcg	25%
Vitamin B-12 (as Cyanocobalamin)	3 mcg	50%
Biotin	600 mcg	200%
Pantothenic Acid (as Calcium d-Pantothenate)	10 mg	100%
Iodine (as Potassium Iodide)	25 mcg	16.5%
Magnesium (as Magnesium Oxide)	20 mg	5%

Zinc (as Zinc Oxide)	15 mg	100%
Copper (as Copper Glutonate)	1 mg	50%
Boron (as Boron Citrate)	1.5 mg	*
Silica (as Silicon Dioxide)	.5 mg	*
MSM (Methylsulfonyl-methane)	250 mg	*
Natural Amino Complex (Lactalbumin)	250 mg	*
L-Cysteine	100 mg	*
L-Methionine	50 mg	*
Choline (as Choline Bitartrate)	125 mcg	*
Inositol	25 mcg	*

* Daily value not established.

- **1 Balanced B-150 B-Complex** tablet by Spring Valley (*they also make other formulas such as B-50 that have the same vitamins, just lower doses*), which contains:

Vitamin B-1 (as Thiamine Mononitrate)	150 mg	10,000%
Vitamin B-2 (as Riboflavin)	150 mg	8,824%
Vitamin B-3 (as Niacinamide)	150 mg	750%
Vitamin B-6 (as Pyridoxine Hydrochloride)	150 mg	7,500%
Folate (as Folic acid)	400 mcg	100%
Vitamin B-12 (as Cyanocobalamin)	150 mcg	2,500%
Biotin	150 mcg	50%
Pantothenic Acid (as d-calcium pantothenate)	150 mg	1,500%
Calcium (as d-calcium pantothenate and dibasic calcium phosphate)	25 mg	3%

- **2 Evening Primrose Oil** softgels by *Spring Valley* ➔ 2,000 mg
- **1 Flax Oil** softgel by *Spring Valley* ➔ 1,000 mg
- **2 Vitamin E** softgels by *Spring Valley* ➔ 800 IU (increased to 2 because of doctor's recommendation)
- **1 GNC Women's Silica** tablet ➔ 11 mg
- **1 Biotin** tablet by *Spring Valley* ➔ 1,000 mcg
- **2 MSM** capsules by *Spring Valley* ➔ 1,000 mg
- **1 Iron** tablet by *Healthy Ideas* ➔ 65 mg (check with your doctor before even thinking about this one – even I plan to schedule a follow-up appointment with my internist to re-evaluate my dosage)

Okay, so this is what I am taking, and I am almost embarrassed to admit the number of pills I take each morning. They are not all related to hair (remember, some are for fibrocystic breast symptoms, dry skin, anemia, and occasional knee pain), but a good number are. Once I started researching, I must admit I got carried away, and after seeing all the products I have tried, you can see *I have that tendency*. As with the products, ***I am obviously not suggesting you take all of these vitamins*** – only ones that you **and your doctor** feel might be helpful in *your* situation. With all I am taking, I am sure you are wondering if there have been any results? Well, after a few months of consistently taking these supplements, I can say that my skin is not as dry as it used to be (*the cover picture, showing my back and arms is proof of that*) – it is softer and smoother, and my nails are growing a little longer. *More importantly*, my new growth seems softer and more manageable, and along with using the Healthier Hair in a Bottle! Oil Spray, I have been able to stretch out my relaxers to 12 weeks and beyond, without excessive breakage. I also think the rate of my hair growth might be a little faster, but I can't conclusively say the results in my hair are all due to the vitamins. *I think having healthier hair is a combination of things – external and internal.* So, once I get my relaxer together and am no longer relaxing and coloring at the same time, I think it will be easier to give you a better assessment. However, for now, I think it is definitely worth the effort, but you must make your own decisions about which vitamins to take and how far above and beyond you want to go. Just check with your doctor first!

5. For the seriously committed hair growers, you might also want to **consider** something known as *protective styling* – wearing styles that protect your ends from exposure *(e.g., buns or updos where the ends are tucked in or covered with a hairpiece or braids, etc.).* I have heard of women getting great results by doing this for long periods. Even though I don't like the whole idea behind protective styling – *pin/cover your hair up, and leave it alone for long periods of time,* I do realize that sometimes there is a need for it, especially during very cold weather. Last winter I did wear my hair in a bun a few times as the weather dropped into the low teens. However, for the most part I wore my hair the way I wanted and threw on a black beret (my mother-in-law gave it to me) as needed to protect my ends from needless exposure. During this time, I also moisturized more, making sure to rub Healthier Hair in a Bottle! Oil Spray and Healthier Hair in a Bottle! Ends Treatment (or Vaseline) onto the ends as often as needed. So there are times where I think we do need to go the extra distance if we are trying to take our hair growth to the next level.

   However, I struggle with the idea of wearing my hair like this for the long-term – intensive moisturizing and covering the hair when needed, yes, but if I can't wear my hair how I want to, I just don't see the fun or enjoyment of having it. I guess I am still caught up in the mental loop that women of other ethnic backgrounds don't have to wear protective styles to grow long hair, and I want us to be free, like them, to wear our hair how we want while growing longer hair! I know some people get great results wearing protective styles on a regular basis, achieving near waist-length hair, and **if you like to wear protective styling, I say that is great and more power to you.** However, there are those of you who can't/don't enjoy wearing your hair in a bun for the long-term. *I know I don't,* and to be honest, the little length I have achieved has not been obtained through the use of consistent protective styling. Believe it or not, wearing our hair in the same style (e.g., pulled back tightly, etc.) for long periods can cause thinning/breakage where the hair is pulled most. So I say *when it makes sense (e.g., you will be out in windy, very cold or hot temperatures for extended periods),* pin it up or cover it up, and always keep it properly moisturized. Otherwise, do your thing wearing low or no-heat styles.

6. **Trim your ends only as needed to remove split-ends, *not as a ritual*.** Over the years, I have read so many articles on hair, and so many of them recommend that we trim our ends every 6-8 weeks. Maybe this is based on the fact that this is about the time many women who relax would visit a salon. It could also be based on the fact that so many of us blow dry, hot curl and flat iron our hair that split-ends are almost inevitable after 6 weeks of heat damage. I am not sure, but after some of the experiences and setbacks I have had after having my hair heavily trimmed by people who said my ends looked good, I am wary of a set time to have your hair trimmed. In fact, now I would not have my ends trimmed unless a stylist actually said they saw split-ends or I thought the ends needed to be evened up for a healthier look. I really believe if you take care of your hair (e.g., follow a healthy hair care regimen similar to the one found in this book), you may be able to go months without trimming. It really depends on how quickly and evenly your hair grows **and** *how well you protect your ends.*

Time to Trim?

If you don't have split-ends, there is not a set time that you **have** to trim your ends. I am starting to think that many stylists trim for reasons other than the presence of split-ends: 1) Out of habit and/or a belief that trimming ends makes the hair grow (*it doesn't – hair grows whether you trim it or not*); 2) The ends are frizzy at the time you come in (could be due to a style such as a plait/braid/twist set, product build-up or humidity); or 3) The ends are uneven (*ends don't have to be evened all at once, it can be done gradually*). Every stylist's motivation and opinion is different, so you never really know, but if your ends are being trimmed for any reason other than removing split-ends, you could be needlessly losing length. For ladies who like a blunt or even cut, this is fine, but if you are trying to grow longer hair, you need to discuss "why" and "how much" will be cut before you allow it to be trimmed. The best thing you can do is **be completely open with your stylist about your concerns and goals**, and work out a trim schedule that works for you. While you are doing this, you may want to also consider having your ends trimmed while your hair is dry, instead of wet (*if you are not doing so already*). My stylist once admitted that it is harder to tell how much to trim when the hair is wet, so she agreed to only trim it dry. If your stylist is not willing to discuss trimming or "not trimming", *professionally and respectfully,* it may be time for you to move on.

So the choice of when to trim is entirely up to us. However, being able to go for long periods without a trim requires a commitment to take extra special care of our hair and ends (e.g., regular shampoos, deep conditioning, minimal brushing and combing, limited heat, satin cap/scarf/pillow cover at night, protective styles as needed, etc.) **and** open communication with our stylist.

Other Trimming Options

Now as I look for a new stylist who is closer to me, I have to admit that I have a strong desire to learn how to trim my own ends. It is hard enough finding someone you can trust to carefully apply chemicals, but to have to trust someone with scissors too – it just feels like too much! For anyone who knows me, I did what I normally do when I am confused about something – *I checked out some books from the library* on hair cutting in case I decide to *try* to do it myself. On a similar note, I am embarrassed to admit that there is yet another product I have been suckered into buying. While I was visiting my mom in GA this summer, I was flipping through channels, and I found myself glued to an infomercial for the *Talavera Split-Ender by RevoStyler.* I know I am such a sucker, but I was almost as excited as when I first saw the infomercial for the Caruso Steam Hair Setter years ago! Just like back then, they had one or two black ladies that they showed towards the end, and by then I was hooked. The infomercial **claimed** that this hand-held hair trimmer "safely and effectively snips away damaged, frizzy split-ends." They also said it "only snips the ends and broken hair fragments along the hair shaft on any length of hair." Now the part that made me write down their website (www.split-ender.com) and number was the claim that this little machine "only trims approximately the last 1/8 inch of the hair … removing the split-ends… leaving strong, freshly trimmed hair behind." They even claimed you don't lose any length, just split-ends! Does this thing work? I don't know, but I am crazy enough to try it on a few sections where no one will notice if it doesn't! It does sound too good to be true and the postage was ridiculously overpriced, *but mine should be arriving any day now, and I can't wait!* I am nervous, but I plan to try it, and share the results (good or bad) on my website.

Bottom line: Whether you go to a stylist, trim yourself or wind up using something strange like the Split-Ender, **split-ends must be trimmed.** *If they are not, the splitting could extend up the entire hair shaft, which will result in severe breakage*, but aside from that, I say **trim with care.**

7. In addition to items 1-6, go even a step further by performing the steps below.

Going a Step Further

To experience major hair growth, you need to get serious about avoiding hair abuse, especially if your hair has already been damaged. You must develop a higher level of consciousness about how you style and treat your hair – you need to think of damage control as much as possible, especially where your ends are concerned. I know this may sound weird or even like I am "hair crazy", but if you want to experience serious hair growth, here are a few reminders from previous chapters:

- *Avoid heat styling tools like the plague*! This includes blow dryers, curling irons, flat irons and electric curlers. Do not blow dry your hair more than once a month, and avoid using the comb/brush attachments. Replace blow drying with wet sets or air drying (see the various drying options in Chapter 4) whenever possible. Also, limit the use of heat styling appliances to no more than one or two times a week. As often as possible replace these appliances with the Caruso Steam Hair Setter, or use wrap styling for straight styles, and overnight sets like a twist or plait/braid set (see Chapter 6 on Styling for alternatives and "how-to" information) for curlier styles. You could also try products such as *Soft Curlers* by *Conair*, *Pillow Soft Rollers* by *Goody, Solar Rollers* by *Nandi* or other soft, self-holding curlers that you can sleep in. Experiment with products like these to create styles ranging from loose curls to spirals. **Bottom line:** *Avoid heat as much as possible*!

- Protect your ends regularly, if not daily. Treat them with some sort of oil protector (see Chapter 5 for recommendations).

- If your hair is relaxed, do not go "*too long*" without a touch-up. The *too long* reference is very subjective – for some women "too long" can be 8 weeks (with the tips given in this book, I hope this is the minimum amount of time you are waiting), 12 weeks or 16 weeks. It depends on how quickly your hair grows and whether you can maintain it without causing excessive breakage. I am encouraging ladies who relax to try to stretch relaxers out as long as possible. Over the last year, I have stretched mine from 5-6 weeks to 12-14 weeks. So the "too long" rule or test is if you cannot comb through the new growth in your hair without pain or the sound of hair popping, it *may* be time. If you are in doubt, or need to drag it out, you can shampoo or do a conditioning rinse on your hair every 3-4 days (see Chapter 3), and use oils such as Healthier Hair in a Bottle! Oil Spray as needed. Avoid combing through the roots if you can help it, and while you wait, either do twist, plait or braid sets or wear your hair in a bun, updo or pony-tail. Make sure you cover your hair at night to avoid losing precious moisture.

- After touch-ups, request wet sets as often as possible (e.g., roller, rods, spiral or straw). Because these styles last at least a week, your hair gets a break from heat styling and combing. These styles can be maintained by finger-combing and wearing a satin scarf or cap overnight. The absence of heat styling and combing will more than make up for the fact that you may miss a shampoo and deep conditioner for one week.

- Avoid back-to-back hair abuse. If your hair had a *rough* week (e.g., a touch-up where your hair was blown dry and hot curled or you hot curled it more than 3 or 4 times), you need to take steps to give your hair a break. Once after getting a touch-up my stylist used a blow dryer to dry my hair completely, which I usually never allow (we did it because of time constraints), and she then hot curled it. After years of avoiding this kind of abuse, I felt guilty, so I decided I will never "allow" this to happen again. To offset this type of abuse, I would massage my scalp with an oil such as Healthier Hair in a Bottle! Oil Spray, and put some on the hair and ends. I might also apply some Healthier Hair in a Bottle! Ends Treatment, and sleep in a satin or plastic cap. If possible, I would also treat my hair to one full week of no-heat styling (e.g., wraps and twist sets) and mostly finger-combing. It may seem like I over-reacted, but I have invested a lot of time in getting my hair to this length, and I refuse to let a few minutes of extra work keep me from reaching my hair goals! As I said, you have to get serious!

- If you don't like sitting under a dryer for sets, instead of blow drying your hair until it is dry, you could ask your stylist to let you sit under the dryer with your hair pinned/clipped or hanging loose until it is ¾ dry. Then ask them to blow the rest dry while combing it with a wide-tooth comb or using a comb attachment. To minimize heat damage and to save up to an hour of time on my total salon visit, I have left a salon with my hair in a pony-tail or pulled loosely back with a headband and the ends slightly bumped or flat ironed. Sometimes I may dress it up with a bang or a side curl in the front, but no more all-over hot curling for me! If this could work for you, try it as often as you are able. One week out of a month give your hair a break – no heat styling, and no combing or brushing. Instead, opt for wraps, twist or plait sets (overnight), straight styles and updos. You could use the Caruso Steam Hair Setter, which uses steam (actually good for hair), not dry heat, during this time. However, it would be better if you just let your hair rest. If you are really serious and ambitious, try to do this for a month!

- If your hair is at a length where you are unable to style it in a way that makes you feel attractive without overusing heat styling tools, why not try "believable looking" hair pieces, extensions or weaves to give your hair a break while you are growing your hair out? Once after my hair was butchered by a new stylist (I never met her, did not know anything about her, did not speak with any references, but I still read a magazine while she trimmed my ends!), I wore a long pony-tail until my hair returned to shoulder length. The object of these "hair helpers" should be to protect your real hair from damage – not to leave it in a worse condition than it was before you had them put in. With this in mind, **I strongly suggest that you do not use glues or bonds on your hair, and do not allow anyone to put extremely tight braids in your hair**. Also, avoid heavy or long braid extensions that pull your hair and scalp. Find a trained weave/extension/braid expert who can help you use these "hair helpers" to help you reach your hair goals. If done right, your hair should look better when they take the braids or extensions out, than it did when they put them in.

- Do not become dependent on braids, weaves or extensions while using them to protect or shelter your hair. After a **set** time, you should take them/it out. You should set a hair goal or length where you will remove the "fake" hair and *wear your own*. Otherwise, you may start to lose, what I call, "real-hair consciousness" after wearing your "fake hair" too long, meaning that you get too used to the "fake hair" and no longer like your appearance without it. Remember the purpose for "adding the hair" – to give your hair a break, *not to replace it*. Long, fake hair is nice, but *your own hair is always better!*

- If you are using the previous tips on young or teenage girls, make sure that you are not damaging their hair or scalp with heavy extensions, braids or ornaments (e.g., beads). It is amazing that a child, or even an adult, with hair that is maybe 4 inches long or shorter would have heavy extensions that are 3 or 4 times that length. This could cause long-term scalp damage, and eventually slow down hair growth. To avoid this, consult with a trained extension/braid expert on the best lengths for your hair, scalp and age.

- Monitor your ends throughout the week – this is especially important for relaxed hair. If relaxed hair is well cared for, the ends should feel smooth and soft, not dry and brittle. If your ends are dry or brittle, whether you have a relaxer or not, moisturize them using the products recommended in Chapter 5 or something similar.

- Monitor your scalp and the overall texture of your hair for dryness. If it is dry, oil the scalp with a rich oil such as Healthier Hair in a Bottle! Oil Spray as needed (once or twice a week) or some other moisturizer for daily treatments. See Chapter 5 for more details. If you notice, I have not really recommended crème moisturizers, and I must say it is because many crème products just coat the hair, but are very rarely absorbed – they often wind up evaporating, leaving your hair dry and poorly protected. I lean more towards natural oils now because they are often more easily absorbed by your hair shaft, protecting from the inside out, without your hair being greasy or weighed down.

Hopefully these tips will get you started on your way to reaching your hair growth goals. However, as a final note, don't become discouraged by the amount of time it may take to get your hair to grow to longer lengths. Although everyone's hair grows at a different rate, *everyone's hair does grow, **and our's is no exception!*** It just takes time to see a noticeable difference. Just as achieving any worthwhile goal takes effort and time, growing hair is no different. As Galatians 6:9 (*New King James Version*) says, "… let us not grow weary while doing good, for in due season we shall reap if we do not lose heart." This same principle applies to our efforts to grow longer hair. Watching hair grow is like watching a child grow, *you often don't notice the day-to-day changes, but they add up to very noticeable growth in the long run.* So as you *diligently* follow the regimen and tips outlined in this chapter, do not lose heart! I guarantee *you will see results, and you will reach your goal* if you are consistent and patient. In the meantime, here's to your future hair-growing success!

CHAPTER 10

PUTTING IT ALL TOGETHER...

I know after reading all I do and recommend to have beautiful, healthier hair (e.g., the *Six-Week Regimen*, Daily Hair Care, Relaxing with Care, etc.) some of you may be thinking, why does it have to be all of that? Well, to be honest it does not have to be "all of that" for *all* of us. Some women are genetically blessed with hair that does not require a lot of maintenance, and there are some women who do not abuse their hair and may not have to "baby" their hair as much. As an example, my cousin Rosalind has had beautiful hair as long as I can remember, and she *seems* to have been blessed with the ability to grow long hair. Looking at her daughter's hair – it is almost waist-length, and it is as healthy looking *as any hair has the right to be*, and she is only 7, so many would argue that they seem to have a genetic predisposition for growing long hair. No one can say for sure. However, Rosalind's good hair care habits over the years (e.g., no curling irons, rare blow drying, as-needed trimming, infrequent combing, no "chair hopping", etc.) prevent her from having to put forth as much effort as I, or the average black woman, may have to. Even when we were young and stupid, she was taking care of her hair – I, on the other hand, was not. The intensive regimen I recommend in this book is mainly for women who abuse or have abused their hair in the past and are trying to get it back to a healthier state, as well as for women who are trying to grow longer hair.

When I use the term "abuse" I am talking about chemical treatments, regular blow drying, frequent use of hot curlers, electric curlers and flat irons, large amounts of combing or brushing, rough handling, infrequent shampooing/conditioning, etc. In general, many of us abuse our hair in a number of these ways on a regular basis. Before now much of it was unavoidable, but this book gives us options to avoid and counteract the abuse our hair may have suffered in the past. However, if you are one of the few black women who has never abused your hair, or if you have been genetically blessed with hair that is naturally long and beautiful, you can pick and choose from the tips and regimens contained in this book to help maintain your hair. **There is something in this book for all of us**, even if it is just air drying techniques or finding low maintenance styles to get you through vacations. If nothing else, you can benefit from all the products I have tried, getting a warm referral on shampoos and conditioners that you might have wanted to try. At a minimum, I hope I can save you money, but the best thing for me would be if the information provided in this book helps black women around the world reach their own personal hair care goals, *whatever they may be*. Now, the absolute best reward that would just have me on my knees praising the Lord would be if I start seeing more of us wearing *our own hair* proudly and achieving results we never were able to reach before! That is my dream, and I think it is one of the reasons I have worked so hard to find answers for myself and to write this second book.

To reap the full benefits of this book, you will need to combine the *Six-Week Regimen* in Chapter 3, or some variation of it, and the daily hair care program in Chapter 5. Other components that will increase your overall hair success can be found in the remaining chapters of this book. Keep in mind that whatever hair care regimen you follow will succeed or fail based on your level of commitment and consistency. I hope this book helps you to adopt or develop a healthier hair care regimen that you can commit to and consistently practice. Doing so will definitely help you have the beautiful, healthy hair you desire. Regardless of the regimen you choose, I wish you much success in life and in your quest for beautiful, healthier hair!